Alan Gartner
Frank Riessman

Self-Help
in the
Human Services

Jossey-Bass Publishers

San Francisco • Washington • London • 1977

SELF-HELP IN THE HUMAN SERVICES
by Alan Gartner and Frank Riessman

Copyright © 1977 by: Jossey-Bass, Inc., Publishers
615 Montgomery Street
San Francisco, California 94111
&
Jossey-Bass Limited
28 Banner Street
London EC1Y 8QE

Library of Congress Catalogue Card Number LC 77-79483

International Standard Book Number ISBN 0-87589-338-4

Manufactured in the United States of America

JACKET DESIGN BY WILLI BAUM

FIRST EDITION

Code 7738

❧❧❧❧❧❧❧❧❧

The Jossey-Bass
Behavioral Science Series

❧❧❧❧❧❧❧❧❧❧❧❧❧❧❧❧

Preface

This book is about self-help, mutual aid* programs in the
human service fields, ranging from Alcoholics Anonymous and other
groups modeled after it to women's and men's consciousness-raising
groups, youth groups, and the various health-oriented groups such
as Reach to Recovery, Emphysema, Inc., Mended Hearts, and The
Stroke Club. Consumer-based self-help programs in mental health,
health, education, and social work will be examined with particular
attention to how they represent new forms of practice that are
productive, nonbureaucratic, and "aprofessional." By the term
aprofessional we mean interventions that are generally based on ex-

* We use the terms *self-help groups, mutual aid groups,* and *mutual
support groups* synonymously throughout this book.

vii

perience, intuition, and common sense, rather than on systematic knowledge.

In the chapters that follow, we (1) examine in depth the major developments and models in self-help practice; (2) offer a theoretical explanation for the mechanisms or processes that may make self-help effective; and (3) discuss issues and future developments (such as the relationship of self-help programs to social change, to preventive health practice, and to professional practice), and the relevance of such groups for low-income underserved populations. We also consider various criticisms of self-help, such as the argument that self-help diverts energy away from the pressure for professional responsibility.

Three major theoretical orientations guide this study. One is that self-help is an example of "aprofessional" practice. We discuss the relationship of aprofessional to professional practice, with particular attention to how the two can or may work together as a dialectic unity, each having its strengths and weaknesses. The second guiding thesis relates self-help to "consumer intensivity," that is, to the role the consumer plays as a *producer of services*. We examine how consumer intensivity is related to increasing the effectiveness and the *quality* of the service. Our third focus is on the "helper-therapy principle," which asserts, in essence, that those who help are helped most (or, giving is getting).

We express our appreciation to Ruth Hunter and Ethel Mingo, who typed and retyped the manuscript and were kind enough to say that the retyping was less than they had expected. Several of our colleagues have read and commented on portions of the manuscript, including Elinor Bowles, Carson Briggs, William Claflin, Colin Greer, Vivian Jackson, David Kaplan, Alfred Katz, Lowell Levin, William Lynch, Mildred Pugh, and Gina Schachter. Also, no one who works in this field can be without debt to Leonard Borman, Gerald Caplan, Zachary Gussow, Mary Conway Kohler, Morton Lieberman, O. Hobart Mowrer, and George Tracy. We appreciate their assistance; of course, the remaining faults are our responsibility.

New York City   ALAN GARTNER
July 1977   FRANK RIESSMAN

Contents

The Authors

ALAN GARTNER is professor, Center for Advanced Study in Education, Graduate School and University Center, City University of New York; and co-director, with Frank Riessman, both of the New Human Services Institute and the National Self-Help Clearing-house. He is publisher of *Social Policy* and editor of the *New Human Services Review*. He has been a faculty member at Queens College and assistant director of the New Careers Development Center at New York University. He was director of the Suffolk County (New York) antipoverty program from 1966 to 1968 and community relations director of the Congress on Racial Equality in 1965–1966.

Gartner received the Ph.D. in urban affairs from the Union Graduate School in 1973; his "Project Demonstrating Excellence" has been published as *The Preparation of Human Service Professionals* (1976). He is also the author of *Paraprofessionals and Their Performance* (1971). His master's degree in history is from Harvard University (1960) and his baccalaureate degree in history from Antioch College (1956).

FRANK RIESSMAN is professor, Queens College, City University of New York; and editor of *Social Policy*. From 1967 to 1973 he was professor at New York University, where he also directed the New Careers Development Center; from 1964 to 1966, at Albert Einstein College of Medicine, where he also directed the Lincoln Hospital Mental Health Aide Training Program; and from 1955 to 1962, at Bard College, where he also chaired the psychology department.

Riessman received the Ph.D. in social psychology from Columbia University in 1955. His master's degree in sociology is from Columbia University (1950) and his baccalaureate degree in psychology from City College of New York (1944). In 1962, he wrote *The Culturally Deprived Child,* which has been revised and reissued as *The Inner City Child* (1976). Other books include *New Careers for the Poor* (with Arthur Pearl, 1965) and *The Mental Health of the Poor* (edited with Jerome Cohen, 1966).

Gartner and Riessman together have written *Paraprofessionals Today: Education* (with Vivian C. Jackson, 1977), *A Full Employment Program for the 1970s* (edited with William Lynch, Jr., 1976), *The New Assault on Equality: I.Q. and Social Stratification* (edited with Colin Greer, 1974), *The Service Society and the Consumer Vanguard* (1974), *After Deschooling, What?* (edited with Colin Greer, 1973), *What Nixon Is Doing to Us: The Great Leap Backwards* (edited with Colin Greer, 1973), and *Children Teach Children* (with Mary Conway Kohler, 1971).

In appreciation for their long and continuing support,
this book is dedicated to our friends and colleagues
Colin Greer, Vivian Copeland Jackson, William Lynch, Jr.,
S. M. Miller, and Marvin Taylor

Self-Help
in the
Human Services

1

Self-Help
and the Human Services

What is the context in which the self-help movement has experienced its current surge of growth? Sidel and Sidel (1976, p. 67) offer the following perspective:

> The self-help and mutual aid movement is a response to a number of different factors in our society which make human services unavailable or unresponsive to those who need them: the pervasiveness of technology and its rate of development; the complexity and size of institutions and communities, with their accompanying depersonalization and dehumanization; the alienation of people from one another, from their communities and institutions, and even from themselves; and the professionalization of much which in the past was done by individuals for themselves or for one another. Self-help groups have made

1

major contributions toward dealing with problems which cannot be dealt with by other institutions in the society, and at the same time have provided people with opportunities for helping roles, roles which have become increasingly difficult to find in our society as more and more helping has been taken over by professionals. Self-help or mutual aid groups provide a mechanism whereby individuals in a collective setting with others who face similar life situations can assume responsibility for their own bodies, psyches, and behavior and can help others do the same. They are the grassroots answer to our hierarchical, professionalized society—to a society which attempts in so many ways to render impotent the individual, the family, the neighbor. Not only are self-help groups providing desperately needed services but they are returning to the individual a feeling of competence and self-respect and they are forging new links, new connections among people.

Although we believe that the self-help approach represents an important advance in human service technology, we do not have a romantic or uncritical attitude toward it. We do not think self-help groups are a cure-all for the problems of our times, nor do we see them as a vanguard force for social change. Indeed, many of the original self-help groups, such as Alcoholics Anonymous, Recovery, Inc., and Synanon, are somewhat authoritarian; in many cases, they substitute an orthodoxy and/or a charismatic all-powerful leader for the professional. While proclaiming great concern for individual independence and autonomy, many of these organizations have fostered lifelong dependence, frequently based on a simple system of beliefs. While criticizing society, they often have blamed the victims—the addicts themselves.

But self-help groups vary enormously, so that some of the newer ones arising in the late 1960s and 1970s—for example, the women's and men's groups, the gay groups, and the social action groups such as the National Welfare Rights Organization, the Center for Independent Living—are not authoritarian, are far more ideological than earlier groups, and are concerned with social change. Then, too, the health groups, such as Mended Hearts, Reach to Recovery, and the groups concerned with ostomies, are not at all involved in the orthodoxies that may characterize the more traditional mental health organizations. The parent groups, such as Parents of Retarded Children, tend to be activist groups much concerned with changing legislation, and certainly have not blamed victims. Given this great variability, we must avoid looking at self-help groups as if they were uniform.

Although we see the self-help approach, if appropriately utilized, as having great potential importance for a marked improvement in the quality of human service practice, our criticisms of much of existing professional practice should not be understood as a rejection of the need for the professional and the professional perspective. Rather, we look to an integration of aprofessional with professional practice in a new amalgam. We view the self-help approach as sometimes providing a challenge to the professional, sometimes a complement or a supplement, sometimes an alternative, and sometimes a way of expanding and enriching professional practice and total human service practice, but rarely as displacing the professional where the professional's expertise is appropriate. This last point is extremely important, because there is a great danger that self-help approaches will be offered, in the context of professional limitations and the overall fiscal crisis, as a substitute or cost-cutting device. Moreover, there is another danger here; namely, that the poor will be given only self-help, and the rich given the professional services as well.

Finally, we see the potential expansion of the human services via the addition and integration of self-help approaches as redistributive, because at the present time the poor, minorities, and the aged do not receive sufficient services. More and better services should particularly benefit these groups.

In essence, we see the self-help movement as arising out of the needs of modern society. One such need is for the expansion and revitalization of services; another grows out of the rapid changes, the loss of traditional authority, the breakdown of institutions, the alienation, anomie, and anarchy that characterize our era. Many of the services provided by self-help units were performed in the past by the family, the church, the neighborhood, and the community. But these institutions have lost much or all of their power; we need new alternatives, new forms. It is in this context that self-help approaches take on their full significance. Finally, we see the self-help movement as having been powerfully affected by the values of the 1960s—by the concern for personal autonomy, participation,

quality of life, human potential, consumer rights, deprofessionaliza-
tion, and decentralization.

History

Several lines of historic development lead to the present
state of the self-help movement. Katz and Bender (1976, p. 15)'
point to the growth of extrafamilial groups during the Industrial
Revolution, and draw the analysis of Kropotkin, the nineteenth-
century Russian revolutionist, that "Man's [and woman's] survival
depended on his [and her] development of attitudes of social cooperation." They note, "in the nineteenth century in England,
Friendly Societies were a significant return to mutual aid principles
in the lower classes' efforts to cope with adverse living conditions"
(Katz and Bender, 1976, p. 17). By the late nineteenth century, the
Friendly Societies had over a million members, and their importance
continued into the twentieth century—several thousand groups in
existence as late as the 1930s.

While Katz and Bender emphasize that the roots of current
self-help groups lie in the Friendly Societies, the consumer cooperatives and the trade unions of England and America, and the ethnic-
based groups of early twentieth-century America, Hurvitz (1976)
sees aspects of early religious movements in current self-help groups.
"The concepts of group confession of guilt-causing experiences,
mutual criticism, and penance were . . . known to early American
religious leaders and laymen" (Hurvitz, 1976, p. 287). The Washingtonians, founded in 1840, applied these concepts to overcome
alcoholism (Sagarin, 1969).

In the 1930s, a number of separate groups of self-helpers
developed. "In 1931, a cooperative self-help movement was begun
in California and other states to combat the effects of unemployment during the Great Depression" (Barish, 1971, p. 1164). These
groups developed into Unemployed Cooperatives, whose members
bartered food, sought to maintain each other's self-respect and independence, and joined together to fight the "Paupers Oath," a
requirement for receipt of public assistance. Responding to a different set of circumstances, in 1936 "former concentration camp
victims formed an organization, Self-Help, to aid newcomers with
jobs, advice, and emotional support" (Barish, 1971, p. 1164).

Also in the 1930s, groups of parents of handicapped children came together, their individual groups ultimately merging into the American Association of Retarded Children and the United Cerebral Palsy Foundation (Barish, 1971, p. 1165). In the same period, the first groups of mental patients developed. Recovery, Inc., was founded in 1937 by Abraham Low, who in 1933 had formed a group among his patients, aimed at preventing relapses and chronic conditions.

The most important development in the 1930s was the founding of Alcoholics Anonymous. Frank Buchman, a Lutheran minister, building on the Lutheran practice of group confession, developed a new movement known as the Oxford Group (later called Moral Rearmament). The Oxford Group worked with college students and emphasized the possibility of a changed life based on "several central assumptions: Men are sinners; men can be changed; confession is a prerequisite for change; and those who have changed must change others" (Hurvitz, 1974, p. 98).

Two alcoholics, both of whom had participated in the Oxford Group, met in Akron in 1933. They applied the principles of the Oxford group and, in an unconscious repetition of the practices of the Washingtonians, recruited others who would acknowledge that they were drunks, come together to hear each other's stories, and help each other. "The founders of AA, who were introduced to public confession in a religious setting, secularized confession; and they formed a fellowship based upon the concept of public confession with one's peers as a way of overcoming behavior that estranged them from their fellows" (Hurvitz, 1974, p. 99). The efforts of "Bill W." and "Dr. Bob" flourished. In 1937 the Akron group had 40 members and in 1939, when they adopted the name Alcoholics Anonymous (AA), there were 100 members (Thomsen, 1975). Following favorable publicity in newspapers and national magazines, AA grew rapidly, and became the model for the other "Anonymous" groups.

The Present

The self-help mode is particularly relevant at the present time because it is economical, nonprofessional, and seemingly effective. Crowded out in the 1960s by larger social movements such as civil rights, antiwar, free speech, and the counterculture, self-help groups seem to be moving toward center stage in the "scarcity" 1970s. Currently, there are over a half million different self-help groups. The National Association for Retarded Children has over 1,300 local units and a membership of more than 130,000. Alcoholics Anonymous, together with its auxiliary groups, has a worldwide membership exceeding 750,000. In a two-county area of New York state alone, among six self-help organizations (Alcoholics Anonymous, Al-Anon, Gamblers Anonymous, Gam-Anon, Overeaters Anonymous, and TOPS), there are over 180 groups. There is a self-help group for nearly every major disease listed by the World Health Organization. There are self-help groups for parents who abuse their children, for isolated older people, the handicapped, drug abusers, Vietnam veterans, the retarded, young people in search of identity and jobs, parents of twins, patients who have had heart attacks or mastectomies, parents of handicapped children, suicide-prone people, smokers, drinkers, overeaters, patients discharged from mental institutions, underachieving children who need tutoring, and parent education groups ("Helpers," 1976).

Actually, of course, the self-help, mutual aid approach has characterized many groups and movements: civil rights, welfare rights, the labor movement, the women's movement, the counterculture, and the student movement. There are also self-help food cooperatives, job-finding groups, energy conservation groups, housing and community groups, and veterans organizations. Our emphasis in the balance of this book, however, will be on human service-oriented mutual aid groups, in which the small group is the central unit. Such self-help groups are defined in a recent book by Katz and Bender (1976, p. 9) as: "Voluntary small group structures for mutual aid in the accomplishment of a specific purpose. They are usually formed by peers who have come together for mutual assistance in satisfying a common need, overcoming a common handicap or life-disrupting problem, and bringing about desired social and/or personal change. The initiators and members of such groups perceive that their needs are not or cannot be met by or through existing social institutions." To this description, we add the following list of features that are critical to self-help groups and that serve to distinguish them from organizations such as unions, cartels, corporation boards, "old boy" networks, and service organizations.

1. Self-help groups always involve face-to-face interactions.
2. The origin of self-help groups is usually spontaneous (not set up by some outside group).
3. Personal participation is an extremely important ingredient, as bureaucratization is the enemy of the self-help organization.
4. The members agree on and engage in some actions.
5. Typically the groups start from a condition of powerlessness.
6. The groups fill needs for a reference group, a point of connection and identification with others, a base for activity, and a source of ego reinforcement.

Many self-help groups provide assistance within an explicit ideological framework; men's and women's groups, for example, as well as groups of exprisoners and parents organized on behalf of children, often expose injustices and attempt to bring about changes in the contemporary American social system.

In addition to being able to provide needed services much more economically than prevailing professional and institutional approaches, there are a number of other reasons why the self-help approach is gaining considerable influence. First, there is a strong antibureaucratic, anti-Leviathan, populist trend in our society. The small group, self-help orientation operates as a countervailing force, reducing alienation and increasing feelings of personal power. Second, self-help approaches are appropriate for a wide range of constituencies, such as women, youth, the aged, and the physically handicapped. Third, self-help activities have proven useful in caring for chronic illnesses (hypertension, diabetes, arthritis, mental illness, cancer, and heart disorders), which afflict 50 percent of our population, especially those who are aging. Fourth, self-help activities try to improve the human services in general, which are inadequate—they do not serve people well and do not reach large numbers of individuals, particularly minorities, rural residents, the aged, adolescents, and the poor.

In the current climate, the traditional services in education, mental health, safety, social services, and the like are severely deprecated for their presumed inefficiency and costliness, but nevertheless *there remains continued pressure for the expansion of all kinds of services.* Legislation now mandates that all educationally handicapped children receive schooling (no longer can these children be ignored or left at home); court decisions are requiring that mental patients receive rehabilitative treatment (no longer can they simply be incarcerated in state institutions); great concern has been expressed regarding the number of abused children (some regard this disturbance as reaching "epidemic" proportions); and research has uncovered the fact that large numbers of people have undetected illnesses such as high blood pressure (some estimates are as high as 19,000,000 for this "silent epidemic") and diabetics (5,000,000). Moreover, national health insurance (if it ever arrives) would operate to expand the health services to be delivered.

Definitions and Taxonomy

Although proponents of self-help are wont to deplore the lack of attention to it, the field is in fact receiving more and more attention. In 1976 alone there appeared two major books (Caplan and Killilea; Katz and Bender), as well as special issues of two journals (*Journal of Applied Behavioral Science* [Lieberman and Borman, 1976b] and *Social Policy* ["Special Self-Help Issue"]). As it is a vast field, it is not surprising that definitions, categorization schemes, taxonomies, and schemes of analysis are rapidly accumulating.

Surely the most exhaustive analysis of the literature of self-help has been done by Killilea (1976). She has cataloged what she describes as the "categories of interpretation" (p. 39).* These include the following social views.

1. *Social assistance, a factor in evolution.* This is the interpretation of Peter Kropotkin, who, as we have noted, emphasized mutual aid as a form of group life that was and is critical for human survival.
2. *Support systems.* This is the formulation of Caplan, who defines

---

* The following uses Killilea's categories (1976, pp. 40–66), while the examples are hers and others.

support systems as "an enduring pattern of continuous or intermittent ties that play a significant part in maintaining the psychological and physical integrity of the individual over time" (Killilea, 1976, p. 7).

3. *A social movement.* Various interpretors of self-help have described it as a social movement, some emphasizing the focus on changing the group's members (Toch, 1965), others focusing on broader societal effect (Gussow and Tracy, undated; Vattano, 1972).

4. *A spiritual movement and a secular religion.* Mowrer (Mowrer and Vattano, 1976) views his Integrity Groups (see Chapter Two) as filling some of the roles that religious groups did in an earlier period, while Synanon now styles itself as a secular religion (Newmark and Newmark, 1976). Of course, there is a spiritual dimension in AA (Hurvitz, 1974), as well as in such offshoots as GA—Gamblers Anonymous (Scodel, 1964). Groups such as Recovery (Wechsler, 1960b) and even the dieting groups (Allon, 1973) also have a religious quality.

5. *A product of social and political forces that shape the helping services.* Several authors (Glaser, 1971; Levine and Levine, 1970; Lewis and Lewis, 1976) have seen self-help as a development in the human services.

6. *A phenomenon of the service society.* Gartner and Riessman (1974) note the development of consumer-intensive services as a central feature of the service society, self-help being a prime example.

7. *An expression of the democratic ideal—consumer participation.* This formulation is strongest in Vattano (1972), although Katz (1972) questions whether the "power to the people" rubric that Vattano uses fits all self-help groups. Dumont (1974) and Sidel and Sidel (1976) offer a more restrained version of this characterization.

8. *Alternative caregiving systems.* For groups and problems that the traditional caregiving system disdains or serves poorly, the self-help groups provide an alternative. This may well be one of the most characteristic aspects of self-help groups.

9. *An adjunct to the professions—a solution to the manpower problem.* In many ways, those groups concerned with "after

care" fit this category. These include Recovery, the ostomy groups, Reach to Recovery, the laryngectomy groups, and the stroke clubs.

10. *An element in a planned care system.* To some extent, mental health programs are now including activities modeled on AA as part of their caregiving system. And at Queens College, City University of New York, workers in mental health agencies are being trained to become organizers and "sponsors" of self-help groups. In the health field, the "activated patient" activities (Sehnert, 1975) and other aspects of "self-care" (Levin, Katz, and Holst, 1976) fit this category.

11. *An intentional community.* Such various drug treatment programs as Synanon (Yablonsky, 1965), Gaudenzia (Glaser, 1971), and Delancey Street (Hampden-Turner, 1976; Sales, 1976) are examples of intentional communities.

12. *A subculture—way of life.* To some extent, each of the self-help groups are subcultures, particularly those that provide a new community for their members (for example, Parents Without Partners and the widow groups), as well as the behavior change groups.

13. *A supplementary community.* Weinberg (1968) describes Little People of America as a supplementary community, as does Weiss (1973) in discussing Parents Without Partners.

14. *A temporary/transitional community.* The various expatient groups in the mental health field play the role of temporary and transitional communities.

15. *Agencies of social control and resocialization.* To some extent, many of the self-help groups act as agencies of social control and resocialization, including all of those concerned with behavior change (AA, GA, the drug groups, and the weight reduction groups), as well as those more formally a part of the criminal justice system (Volkman and Cressey, 1963).

16. *Expressive/social influence groups.* Self-help groups serve both to meet the self-interest of their members ("expressive") and to influence the larger society ("instrumental"). Gussow and Tracy (undated) point to this dualism in their division of self-help groups in health into Type I and Type II (see Chapter Three).

17. *Organizations of the deviant and stigmatized.* To some extent, the tendency to destigmatize is a characteristic of all of the self-help groups, although, of course, the extent of the stigma varies. Sagarin (1969) has identified this as the central characteristic of the groups, and Steinman and Traunstein (1976, p. 356) note that a majority of the members of the self-help groups they studied stated that their most important objective was to change the public's definition of their condition from "deviant" to "different."

18. *A vehicle to aid coping with long-term deficits and deprivations.* The various health groups concerned with ostomates, laryngectomees, and mastectomees fit this categorization, as does the Center for Independent Living (Kirshbaum, Harveston, and Katz, 1976).

19. *A vehicle to aid coping with life cycle transitions.* La Leche League, Parents Without Partners, and the various widow groups all serve this function. It is interesting to note that these groups are almost exclusively female.

20. *A therapeutic method.* Each of the various groups has its "way," ranging from AA's "Twelve Steps" to the Integrity Group's "Ten Commitments." Antze (1976) describes this way as the unique "ideology" of the groups, while Hurvitz (1974) has conceptualized an entire alternative therapeutic modality that he says characterizes peer self-help psychotherapy groups (see Appendix B of this book).

None of the other observers of self-help activities has developed as an elaborate a categorization as has Killilea. There are, however, a number of more discrete categorization schemes that serve to further elucidate some of the key characteristics of self-help groups. Sagarin (1969), in the context of deviance management, distinguishes between groups that focus on self-reforming and on relinquishing the stigmatizing behavior (such as AA, GA, and Recovery) and groups that seek to reform the norms of society (such as Mattachine, Bilitis, other gay liberation groups, and, to some extent, the various women's groups and the Gray Panthers). Related to this contrast is the categorization according to the extent the groups accept societal norms; here, again, groups such as AA, GA, and Recovery fall at the high end of the scale, while groups such as Synanon, the women's groups, and the social action groups fall at the low end. Of course, there is the concomitant matter of whether the group feels "their problem" to be rooted in the individual (be it by willful act or as a consequence of a disease) or to be rooted in society's attitudes or actions.

Katz and Bender (1976) also propose a useful typology of self-help organizations: (1) groups that are primarily focused on self-fulfillment or personal growth (for example, Recovery, Inc.); (2) groups that are primarily focused on social advocacy (for example, the Committee for the Rights of the Disabled); (3) groups whose primary focus is to create alternative patterns for living (for example, women's and gay liberation) and (4) "outcast havens" or "rockbottom" groups that provide a refuge for desperate people who are attempting to secure personal protection from the pressure of life and society (for example, the X-Kalay Foundation in Vancouver, British Columbia).

The Professional Issue

Implicit in the self-help thrust is a profound critique of professionalism. Traditional professional models, whether in psychotherapy, education, or other services, are seen as outmoded for modern needs, and the traditional relationship between professionals and consumers is not only inconsistent with the participatory ethos emerging out of the 1960s, but also seems to be correlated with inefficient and ineffective service delivery. Self-help mutual aid groups have developed, in large measure, because of the unwillingness and inability of professional organizations to deal with these and other problems, and because of such organization's overly intellectualized orientation, excessive credentialism, and limited reach in regard to various populations. Traditionally, the professions have been characterized by (1) control of entry into the occupation; (2) colleague rather than client orientation in terms of standards; (3) an occupational code of ethics; and (4) a "scientific-theoretical" basis for occupational activity. In exchange for the promise by professions to act for the public good (the outcome of which is hard to evaluate), the professionals have been given very considerable power in areas such as entry into and exclusion from the field, evaluation, standards setting, and remuneration (Gartner, 1976). While the power of the professionals has somewhat eroded in the past decade, for the most part that power remains intact, and, more fundamentally, the erosion of their power has not brought into question the basis of that power.

We suggest that in the human services the very basis of the power of the professionals is ill-founded. One basic characteristic of the human services is the fact that they should not be, as the professional authority model purports, centered on the professional; rather, they should be seen as centered on the client. In the services, the consumer (the client) is the key producer. The result of the service provision—be it by a doctor, teacher, or social worker—is not simply a benefit to the consumer. Ultimately, it is the patient, student, or client who produces his or her own health, learning, or well-being. The teacher teaches, but it is the student who must do the learning.

A second central characteristic of the human services is the major extent to which the consumer serves himself or herself. For example, it has been estimated that 85 percent of health care is self-care (Levin, Katz, and Holst, 1976); similarly, much of what we learn is learned on our own without being taught.

Both of these basic characteristics of the human services are subordinated in the professional-dominated model. Of course, marginal concessions of authority by the professionals have occurred in response to pressure from consumer groups and others. However, these concessions have left the structure of professional dominance intact, and, more importantly, there has been no questioning of the basic model. What is called for is a fundamental restructuring of the basic nature of the human services. The consumer, not the professional, should stand at the center. The consumer, rather than the professional, should define both the profession's "turf" and its terms of activity. Everett Hughes, the distinguished sociologist of the professions, once defined a "quack" as one who satisfies his clients, but not his peers—a client-centered practice would label as a quack one who satisfies his or her professional peers, but not his or her clients!

The entire ethos of the professional orientation is very different from the self-help orientation, which is much more activistic, consumer centered, informal, open, and inexpensive. The self-help approach stresses the aprofessional dimension—the concrete, the subjective, the experiential, and the intuitive—in contrast to the professional emphasis on distance, perspective, reflection, systematic knowledge, and understanding.

In our view, both the professional and the aprofessional have valuable attributes in an integrated practice—each is needed. The self-help orientation, like the paraprofessional orientation of the 1960s (see Pearl and Riessman, 1965), provides the needed aprofessional dimension to balance a practice that has become overly professionalized. This is not to reject the value of professional knowledge, system, organization, or evaluation—all of which are needed to balance the self-help perspective. But the two together could provide far better human service practice, particularly because of the unique features of the human services.

A Unique Dimension of the Human Services

We have already noted that human services should be client centered. Human service work has another highly unique aspect that is frequently overlooked. This is the fact that much work in this field can be performed by people with no formal systematic knowledge or training; rather, their ability or skill rests on their humanness, their feeling for people, their caring, their everyday, down-to-earth experience and common sense, their spontaneity, their availability, and their time. This is one of the main reasons why nonprofessionals, paraprofessionals, indigenous community residents, volunteers, neighborhood support givers, and self-help groups can be effective. There are drawbacks, of course, to this concrete, intuitive, human-based intervention. Frequently, overidentification, uncontrolled subjectivity, and just plain inadequate knowledge seriously limit the value of the care. Thus, the role of training, supervision, and professional knowledge is important for a balanced, well-developed, human service practice. But the human-based dimension is also critical in counterbalancing the weaknesses of professional practice that are derived from its distancing and elite character, and (sometimes) from the limitations of its knowledge base. The human emphasis allows the aprofessional practitioner to reach the client on the client's own turf, and the potential identification of aprofessional with client (which need not always be sympathetic or unambivalent) provides a valuable avenue of contact.

The significance of the aprofessional human dimension to human service practice is far-reaching. First of all, the input of the unskilled human service producer is far less expensive than that of the professional. Second, this input is not only useful to the recipient of the service (a truth currently unrecognized by the professional model, but equally applicable to both professional and aprofessional help), but is also useful to the giver, the helper. In a program of human services balanced between professional and aprofessional modes, the professional input could be used much more efficiently and judiciously than is the current practice. Frequently, tasks are overprofessionalized—professional skills are used when they are not needed and may even be inappropriate.* Since human service needs are almost infinite, it is important, in a long-range view, to recognize that we do not need an infinite amount of professional skill to deal with these needs, but rather that we need an efficient system combining the professional with the aprofessional.

Much contemporary criticism of the human service practice argues that the professional practitioner does too much *to* and *for* the client. In addition, there are a variety of other limitations of the human services to which the self-help approach may provide a useful antidote. One of the most central is the lack of productivity in the human services.

Self-Help and the Productivity Crisis

Traditionally, we have thought of productivity as a function of technology: The more machinery, the more efficient production will be. This has certainly been characteristic of the manufacturing of goods. On the other hand, the services are labor intensive; they use a high proportion of labor or human power and a correspondingly low proportion of machinery or capital in order to produce the service product, whether that product be education, health, safety, or personal services. To make the services more

* A central aspect of current developments in health self-care is enabling the consumer to know when to and when *not* to contact a doctor (Sehnert, 1975).

efficient, it has seemed natural to try to mechanize them more; that is, to apply machinery so that they will perhaps become more like manufacturing. In health, education, and many other service industries, however, unlike in goods production, the consumer frequently plays an important part in effecting productivity, as Victor Fuchs (1968) points out. And Gartner and Riessman (1974, p. 76) note that "in the supermarket, laundromat, the consumer actually works, and in the doctor's office the quality of medical history the patient gives might influence significantly the productivity of the doctor. Productivity in banking is affected by whether the clerk or the customer makes out the deposit slip—and whether it is made out correctly or not. Thus the knowledge, experience, honesty, and motivation of the consumer affects service productivity."

Thus we may need to develop a new classification that might be termed *consumer intensive*—the more the productivity of the provider depends on consumer behavior, the more consumer intensive is the industry or activity. Some services can be seen as both labor intensive (that is, little capital or machinery) and consumer intensive; health outside the hospitals would be one such service, social services another. Other services might be consumer intensive and capital intensive; for example, banking, insurance, and computer-based instruction.

Implicit in this point is the idea that the consumer's involvement adds to the productivity of the service system and of the professional provider (if the latter is involved). This productivity can be enhanced by the fuller use of the consumer, whether as children teaching children, in peer counseling, in self-help organizations, as doctors teaching patients how to make self-examinations, as teachers involving children in their own learning, and in practically all group therapy. In other words, while consumer intensivity is an essential characteristic of all services, it can be greatly increased by organizing these services so as to more fully involve the consumer as producer; thus, one can say that a service is *more* consumer intensive to the degree that the consumer provides a greater portion of the service and the professional provider provides a lesser portion of it.

A derivative of this point is the fact that the more com-

Another set of dangers relates to the consequences for the consumer:

1. When self-help is emphasized, a particularly pernicious form of victim blaming is possible.
2. Persons engaged in mutual aid activities may get participation but not help.
3. Where cures are available and where professional expertise appropriate, involvement with self-help may divert attention from such resources.
4. Dependence may be encouraged—the self-help participant may come to believe that only by remaining in the group can he or she stay healthy.

As the role of the consumer expands, both in self-help activities and in other human services activities, the extent of these dangers are likely to be mitigated. We believe, however, that the struggles with these dangers are ongoing.

Conclusion

Groups and individuals who presently do not receive adequate services may be reached by local self-help approaches, and self-help may also be used to provide better services to people who are now being served inadequately. The self-help approach also leads to much greater emphasis on a consumer-oriented system than on the currently overprofessionalized one. It works strongly against making consumer or clients dependent and is much more activating, for example, than our current welfare system or much of our health system. And self-help increases accountability because it is much more determined by consumer or customer satisfaction than by more autonomous peer (professional) criteria.

In today's economic context, in which extremely mechanical quantitative measures are utilized for increasing productivity (such as requiring that an instructor teach more students, rather than concentrating on whether they learn more), the self-help approach may offer advances in productivity without equivalent cost increases. This is extremely important because even if we were to shift resources from other areas, such as the military sector, we would be wise to conserve our resources and utilize them efficiently, particularly in the light of the overall environmental crisis. An economical approach to human service resources calls for a more selective use of highly trained and costly professional inputs and a much greater utilization of aprofessional and self-help resources.

The question now is whether the self-help orientation can provide more consumer power and better quality and more efficient delivery of services—especially for those on the lower rungs of the socioeconomic ladder, for whom service system inadequacies and societally imposed powerlessness are painfully characteristic of daily life. The rising expectations of the 1960s regarding the quality of life, along with the recognition of the rights of all people to needed services, has not been entirely reversed in the scarcity 1970s. The self-help approach is likely to be one important avenue for responding positively to these developments.

2

Self-Help
and Mental Health

Self-help groups are most extensive in the mental health field. Here the experience of the individual offers greatest assistance to another and, as well, where the professional interventions, particularly regarding addictive behaviors, offer the least help.

We begin the chapter with Alcoholics Anonymous, the largest of the self-help mutual aid groups, and then turn to those groups modeled upon or derived from it. We turn next to groups of former mental patients. Following a description of groups of people who live with those who have a problem—an alcoholic parent or spouse, a congenitally ill child, we close the chapter with consideration of persons who are undergoing role transitions—the newly widowed, parents without partners, new mothers and youth.

The "Anonymous" Groups

It is the "anonymous" groups, particularly Alcoholics Anonymous, that most people think of when discussing self-help mutual aid. Not only do they represent the largest single set of such groups but they also present the most coherent and consistent set of principles. The power of these principles is seen not only in the continuing growth of AA but in the adoption of the model, sometimes intact, by groups concerned with other behavior disorders—gambling, narcotics, overeating, child abuse, and the like. (See Table 1.)

Table 1. The "Anonymous" Groups.

Group	Year Founded	Numbers of Clubs/ Chapters	Size of Membership
Alcoholics Anonymous	1935	26,967	578,007
Addicts Anonymous	1974	NA*	50
Al-Anon	1954	7,500	120,000
Alateen	1957	1,000	NA*
Emphysema Anonymous	1965	7	2,000
Fatties Anonymous	1967	1	200
Gam-Anon	1962	140	1,400
Gamblers Anonymous	1957	210	4,500
Mothers Anonymous	1961	40	600
Narcotics Anonymous	1953	250–300	NA*
Neurotics Anonymous	1965	300	600
Overeaters Anonymous	1960	474	NA*
Parents Anonymous	1969	450	4,000

* NA—data not available.
Source: AA membership figure from *A Brief Guide to Alcoholics Anonymous* (1975); information on Narcotics Anonymous from *Narcotics Anonymous* (1976); information on Parents Anonymous from Lieber (1976); all other information from Gussow and Tracy (1973).

Alcoholics Anonymous. In many ways, it is appropriate to begin a description of self-help groups with Alcoholics Anonymous.

Founded in 1935, AA is the oldest of groups currently in existence (W. [Bill], 1957; Thomsen, 1975; Barish, 1971). It is the largest self-help organization—one study estimated 18,612 AA groups in 1972 and AA itself reports 26,967 groups in 1975 (Gussow and Tracy, undated). It is also the group most written about—in 1973, Phillips published a sixty-three-page annotated bibliography of writings about AA. AA has been both the model of self-help for many and the spawning ground of at least two dozen other closely related groups,* including Gamblers Anonymous, Narcotics Anonymous, Neurotics Anonymous, Parents Anonymous, and Prison Families Anonymous, as well as AA "auxiliary" groups such as Al-Anon and Alateen. The involvement of children of alcoholics is sufficiently extensive in AA activities that the Nineteenth International Conference of Young People in Alcoholics Anonymous, held in Philadelphia in 1976, was attended by over a thousand delegates. AA has such an impressive record of success, that the World Health Organization has called it "the greatest therapeutic organization in the world" (Park, 1976, p. 407).

AA offers the most vivid expression of one set of characteristics of self-help groups: the focus on behavior; the attention to symptoms; the importance of the role of the group and the value of the knowledge and experience of the "oldtimers" (long-time members); and the viewing of the problem (alcoholism) as chronic (the alcoholic is viewed as never being cured). Although its distinguishing features are by no means common to all self-help groups,† AA does share with many such groups an additional set of characteristics, including a high degree of authoritarianism; a

---

* The following list of "Anonymous" groups is no doubt incomplete, as new groups are formed frequently: Cancer Anonymous, Checks Anonymous, Convicts Anonymous, Crooks Anonymous, Delinquents Anonymous, Disturbed Children Anonymous, Divorcees Anonymous, Dropouts Anonymous, Fatties Anonymous, Gamblers Anonymous, Migraines Anonymous, Mothers Anonymous, Narcotics Anonymous, Neurotics Anonymous, Overeaters Anonymous, Parents Anonymous, Parents of Youth in Trouble Anonymous, Prison Families Anonymous, Psychotics Anonymous, Recidivists Anonymous, Relatives Anonymous, Retirees Anonymous, Rich Kids Anonymous, Schizophrenics Anonymous, Sexual Child Abusers Anonymous, Skin Anonymous, Smokers Anonymous, Stutterers Anonymous, Suicide Anonymous, and Youth Anonymous.

† For an example of the heated disagreement created by lumping together self-help groups of differing value orientations, see Katz (1972).

form of blaming the victim; acceptance of societal stigmatization
(Sagarin, 1969; Goffman, 1963) and the need for behavior reform
by the individual; and "acceptance of the prevailing, dominant
cultural and social values" (Katz and Bender, 1976, p. 39). Speaking of a variety of self-help groups, including AA, Caplan (1974,
p. 21) notes that they are "explicitly authoritarian. Members are
expected to adhere to a strict code of conduct, centering of course
on drug abstinence. They are kept under careful surveillance and
they are severely judged for backsliding, which is punished by public
condemnation and shaming. [*] To me, they also resemble religious
orders in their social structure and controls. All of these institutions
have in common a well-defined mission to train members and support them in a disciplined new style of life; they combine an
authoritarian hierarchy with an open-ended upward mobility system
that balances punitive sanctions for nonconformity with the very
tangible rewards of unlimited promotion for merit."

In the past few years, while maintaining its basic position
of focusing exclusively upon its members and their day-to-day problems, AA seems to be reaching out more to the broader community.
For example, AA World Services has been publishing pamphlets
such as *AA: A Community Resource for Coping with a National
Health Problem,* which had a 1975 print run of 100,000; *If You
Are a Professional, AA Wants to Work with You,* a 1973 print
run of 150,000; and *Alcoholism Is a Management Problem,* a 1974
print run of 125,000.

The growth of AA is a tribute to its effectiveness. One observer noted a rise in membership between 1939 and 1947 from
100 members to more than 40,000 (Ritchie, 1948). Since 1947,
the number of AA groups has increased by about 3 percent a year,
growing from 1,664 groups to the 1975 total of 26,967, with
578,007 members. The extent of AA and the involvement of its
members is partially illustrated by the fact that in New York City
alone there are some 1,200 AA group meetings a week (Intergroup
Association of Alcoholics Anonymous of Greater New York, 1976).

The AA format has remained stable over its forty years. The

---

* It seems more accurate to describe the reaction to a relapse from
sobriety as one of intense concern and active efforts to help the individual
return to sobriety.

individual, whose anonymity is preserved, is held responsible for his (75 percent of the members are men) conduct, while he invests faith in the group's power to help achieve day-by-day abstinence. The "Twelve Steps" and "Twelve Traditions" of AA provide a guideline for individual behavior (available from Alcoholics Anonymous World Services, Box 459, Grand Central Station, NY 10017).

Twelve Suggested Steps of Alcoholics Anonymous

1. We admitted we were powerless over alcohol—that our lives had become unmanageable.
2. Came to believe that a Power greater than ourselves could restore us to sanity.
3. Made a decision to turn our will and our lives over to the care of God as we understood him.
4. Made a searching and fearless moral inventory of ourselves.
5. Admitted to God, to ourselves and to another human being the exact nature of our wrongs.
6. Were entirely ready to have God remove all these defects of character.
7. Humbly asked Him to remove our shortcomings.
8. Made a list of all persons we had harmed, and became willing to make amends to them all.
9. Made direct amends to such people wherever possible, except when to do so would injure them or others.
10. Continued to take personal inventory and when we were wrong promptly admitted it.
11. Sought through prayer and meditation to improve our conscious contact with God, as we understood Him, praying only for knowledge of His will for us and the power to carry that out.
12. Having had a spiritual awakening as the result of these steps, we tried to carry this message to alcoholics, and to practice these principles in all our affairs.

The Twelve Traditions of Alcoholics Anonymous

1. Our common welfare should come first; personal recovery depends upon AA unity.

2. For our group purpose there is but one ultimate authority—a loving God as He may express Himself in our group conscience. Our leaders are but trusted servants; they do not govern.

3. The only requirement for AA membership is a desire to stop drinking.

4. Each group should be autonomous except in matters affecting other groups or AA as a whole.

5. Each group has but one primary purpose—to carry its message to the alcoholic who still suffers.

6. An AA group ought never endorse, finance or lend the AA name to any related facility or outside enterprise, lest problems of money, property, and prestige divert us from our primary purpose.

7. Every AA group ought to be fully self-supporting, declining outside contributions.

8. Alcoholics Anonymous should remain forever nonprofessional, but our service centers may employ special workers.

9. AA, as such, ought never be organized; but we may create service boards or committees directly responsible to those they serve.

10. Alcoholics Anonymous has no opinion on outside issues; hence the AA name ought never be drawn into public controversy.

11. Our public relations policy is based on attraction rather than promotion; we need always maintain personal anonymity at the level of press, radio and films.

12. Anonymity is the spiritual foundation of all our traditions, ever reminding us to place principles before personalities.

Although each of the Twelve Steps, and the Twelve Traditions are considered important, it is the first step, admission of the hold alcohol has over one's life, which is most important, the one AA members "must" accept. The last step, involving the helping of others, is the culmination of the process. In effect, the Twelve Steps indicate AA's position "that although the individual is powerless over alcohol, he can overcome his problem through self-appraisal, disclosure and responsible behavior" (Vattano, 1972, p. 10).

Not surprisingly, AA has been the self-help group most critically examined. And its members are sensitive to the various charges that have been leveled against it, as the following presentation made by an AA leader at a self-help conference illustrates (cited in Borman, 1975, p. 55).

I would first like to comment on what Alcoholics Anonymous is not. It does not solicit members from bars. We don't go in the bars to get people to join AA. It doesn't keep membership records or case histories. It doesn't engage in sponsored research. [*] It doesn't offer spiritual or religious services. There is no attempt to control its members. It does not engage in education or propaganda about alcohol. It does not provide housing, food, clothing, jobs, money, or other social services. It does not accept any money for its services or any contributions from non-AA sources. They don't ask you to sign anything when you first come in. They don't ask what social position you have. They don't ask what intellectual ability you have. They just stretch out their hand and say, "Please come back." Thank you.

Three pairs of seeming contradictions characterize AA. First, the participant is told that he is helpless to overcome alcoholism—yet he must take responsibility for his actions. Second, the individual is told that he is free—yet the Twelve Steps prescribe a philosophy and a set of behaviors. Third, while responsibility is focused on the individual, it is the group that provides the central vehicle for AA's work. This combination of allowing the individual to see himself as helpless while at the same time seeing AA as having *the* way to energize him as part of the group to cope with his alcoholism may be the feature that makes AA effective.

Looking at the role of ideology in self-help groups, particularly in AA, Antze emphasizes the freeing of the alcoholic's excessive "sense of agency. To absorb the AA message is to see oneself much less as the author of events in life, the active fighter and doer, and much more as a person with the wisdom to accept limitations and wait for things to come" (Antze, 1976, p. 332). Antze identifies the ways in which AA's ideology achieves this end, noting that the belief that alcoholism is a permanent disease both removes drinking from the voluntary sphere—the alcoholic simply cannot drink at all—and it lifts the burden of blame from the individual. The belief

---

* In 1968, AA World Services did sponsor a sample survey of AA members (Morris, 1970).

that only when he "hits bottom" will the alcoholic be able to accept that when he is alone he is not in control dovetails with the belief that as the self becomes less of an agent in daily life, there is a "higher power" that fills this role. And, finally, "Twelfth Stepping"— that is, carrying AA's message to other alcoholics—serves both to provide a constant object lesson in the seriousness of alcoholism and the need for constant vigilance, and, where efforts succeed, to "provide continuing personal demonstrations of the power of AA, while failure [can be] easily written off to the prospect's unreadiness" (Antze, 1976, p. 333).

Gamblers Anonymous. Similar to AA in both ideology and procedures is Gamblers Anonymous, which was established in 1957 by AA members. Here, too, the group plays an important role, anonymity is preserved, an official credo delineates the individual's responsibility for his gambling (again, the bulk of the members are men), and members subscribe to a variant of the AA Twelve Steps. As with AA meetings, those of Gamblers Anonymous follow a simple and generally unvarying format. The credo is read aloud, and members comment on it; each member is called on to give a "weather report"; there is a brief prayer; and the formal meeting then ends, often followed by an informal discussion session.

The "weather report" provides the most distinctive feature of the meeting. Scodel (1964, p. 117) gives the following example.

I'm Jack R., compulsive gambler. I'm a compulsive loser too, but I don't lose no more because I don't gamble no more. I want to tell you that six months ago when I first walked through that door, I had reached the depths of degradation. To give you an example how low I was, my wife was in the hospital having a baby, and I was holed up in some stinkin,' petty larceny joint over in Emeryville playing lowball. I was in hock up to my ears, I had lost all my self-respect, I couldn't look anybody in the face, I was the kind of guy that if you had a sawbuck to your name, I'd figure a way of conning you out of $9.98. I was always trying for the big score, and later I was trying just to get even and the harder I tried, the more I kept getting in deeper and deeper. And what the hell was this big score anyway? I made it a couple of times so what did I do with the money? I blew it, I had to blow it, it wasn't real money, it was Mexican money, strictly counterfeit. My wife never even got a dress or a pair of shoes out of it. I mean, I was in bad shape. I was writing lousy checks, thank God I was able to cover them in time, but for the Grace of God, I'd be in durance vile right now. But you know the routine as well as I do, we're all the same, we've all gone the same route. But things are different now since I've joined GA. I'm not out of hock yet, but I can see that silver lining up there in all those clouds. I don't know what it is, maybe it's just coming to these meetings, maybe it's some higher power, but I'm getting serenity, some peace of mind now. Like Harry G. says, "Progress is our Most Important Product," and I'm progressing all the time. Just lately, after an absence of many, many years, my wife and I rejoined the church of our faith. When I joined GA, I didn't even come on my own, I had to square a beef with my wife, I admit it, but I decided she was right. I looked in the mirror one morning and I said to myself, "Schmuck, what are you doing with your life?" I know I'm still a compulsive gambler, if I start staying away from here, I'll be right back where I started from. But I take it one day at a time, I haven't gambled in the last twenty-four hours and tomorrow's another day. That's my weather report.

Many of the features of the "weather report" are common to all of the anonymous groups: the participant having hit bottom; the self-degradation; the lack of alternatives; the value of the group and its way being affirmed both for the speaker (and other old-timers) as well as for the benefit of newcomers; and the inability of the individual to behave adequately without the group. These commonalities are no accident, for, as with Gamblers Anonymous, Narcotics Anonymous and Neurotics Anonymous were founded by AA members and have adopted the Twelve Steps and the Twelve Traditions. Indeed, the first lines of the Neurotics Anonymous basic brochure states, "Neurotics Anonymous does for the mentally and emotionally disturbed individual (Neurotic) what Alcoholics Anonymous does for the alcoholic. It operates exactly as does AA" (*Neurotics Anonymous*, 1966, p. 3). And Prison Families Anonymous, with Prison Children Anonymous, was founded by former members of Al-Anon.

Parents Anonymous. Although it shares a common name with AA and incorporates some of its notions, Parents Anonymous (PA) is in many ways different from the other anonymous groups.

It was launched in 1969, when Jolly K., then a twenty-nine-year-old mother of two was receiving mental health counseling from Leonard L. Lieber, met with Lieber and another abusing parent from Lieber's caseload (*I Am A Parents Anonymous Parent,* 1974, pp. 6–7). These three established a group that by 1974 had grown to seventy chapters. Then, in June 1974, PA received a grant from the Office of Child Development (OCD) in the U.S. Department of Health, Education and Welfare. Two years later, there were 450 chapters, with over 4,000 parents attending weekly meetings (Lieber, 1976, p. 3). With the support of the OCD grant, some 10,000 letters were answered, a twenty-four hour toll-free WATS line installed, a newsletter (*Frontiers*) published for a mailing list of over 18,000, additional pamphlets and brochures produced, and public service promotion spots developed. Like other organizations that have been funded externally, PA is now looking "to new funding sources, including corporations, foundations, and individuals. Small donors, big donors, donors of special projects" ("The Honeymoon Is Almost Over," 1975, p. 1). One of the major differences between AA and PA is that AA refuses any support from nonalcoholics—and limits the contributions of alcoholics, as well.

Another difference is in the role of professionals. As we have noted, Lieber, a psychiatric social worker, was a cofounder (with Jolly K.) and is now PA's National Administrator. Four of the ten officers and members of PA's Board of Directors are doctors or social workers, and there is a thirteen-person Advisory Council, all but one of whom is an M.D. or Ph.D.; the lone nondoctor is a member of the family that initially funded PA and is one of only two females on the council.

Beyond their leadership role at the national level, professionals are intimately involved in the local PA group. In order to launch a PA group, according to PA's elaborately precise, overtly directive *Chapter Development Manual,* each chapter must have a sponsor, who "should be a professional person in the mental health field who has a profound respect for the self-help concept" (*Parents Anonymous,* 1974, p. 4). In a careful distinction, the *Manual* notes a preference among social workers for those who are licensed social workers (as is Lieber), in contrast with those who merely have M.S.W. degrees (Master of Social Work). Sponsors attend the weekly PA meetings and provide advice to the chairperson (who is a member of PA). The *Manual* describes the relationship between chairperson and sponsor as that of "an active parent-with-a-supportive-grandparent," who provides advice to members during the meetings and through telephone contact between meetings.

As with the other anonymous groups, PA members acknowledge the presence of a problem and the need for help; plan to take one step, one day at a time; agree not to divulge the names of other members; and take responsibility for their own behavior. Parents Anonymous is thus a "mixed" organization. It combines many features of the other anonymous groups with characteristics abhorrent to them, such as outside funding and integral involvement of professionals. It will be interesting to observe PA's progress after June 1977, when its OCD grant expires, to see whether its momentum continues (from 70 chapters in 1970 to 450 in 1974), and, more importantly, to see whether its apparent popularity continues.

Synanon and Related Groups

Many of the characteristics of the "Anonymous" groups also typify several of the drug addiction programs. Caplan (1974, pp. 21–22) offers a preliminary description of these programs: "Organizations that help their members break a noxious habit—alcoholism, drug abuse, smoking, or overeating—offer not only individual and group counseling in dealing with the problems involved and particularly anticipatory guidance from oldtimers in preparing for expectable difficulties, but they also extend individual ego strength by group sharing of the miseries and discomforts of withdrawal symptoms. In addition, they provide a community in which friendships can develop to provide a new meaning to life; also, social and recreational activities can take place that offer a distraction from unsatisfied cravings." In this chapter we will discuss Synanon, its East Coast counterpart, Daytop Village, and Delancey Street, a San Francisco offshoot.

Just as AA is the prototypical anonymous organization, so Synanon is the prototype of the alternative community program in the drug field. It is not large—there are presently some 1,500 residents at five California locations (Borman, 1975, p. 58). Synanon is, however, the most written about of such organizations (Collier, 1967; Enright, 1970; Yablonsky, 1965; Weppnea, 1973; Ofshe,

1974; Goffman, 1963) and the most controversial (Newmark and Newmark, 1976).

Founded in 1958 by Charles Dederich, an alcoholic who, while an AA member, rejected AA's assumption of a God-directed basis, Synanon incorporates many features of AA. Here, again, the participants have reached bottom, they can expect no cure, and they must take responsibility for their own behavior. The group (here, the whole Synanon community) offers *the* way to acceptable behavior. The use of taped speeches by Dederich and other oldtimers serves much the same purpose as the recital of AA's "Twelve Steps," while the "Synanon Game" builds on GA's "weather report."

The Game, however, is a group exercise. Characterized by withering personal confrontations designed to force all participants to be totally honest about their previous behavior and, thus, to take responsibility for their present and future actions, the Game serves the same purpose as the self-declarations of the "Anonymous" groups. Other functions of the Game grow out of the fact that Synanon is a total community. "The Synanon Game is the core of Synanon, basic to its management, its rehabilitation process, and its general 'people business' " (Simon, 1976, p. 1). It serves a governmental role, a role as an art form, as education, as sport, as a communications and business management tool, as well as a therapeutic technique. At one level, the Game acts as a counterbalance to the hierarchical structure of Synanon's governance. In the metaphor of Synanon, it is the "circle" in balance against the "triangle." Here all are equal, in that anything (except violence) goes, and what is said in the Game is not supposed to be used against a person outside of it. Coming to Synanon to study the Game for a Harvard doctoral dissertation, Simon remained, becoming a Synanon resident and, after Dederich, the recognized expert on the Game. He contrasts life in the Game with "on the floor" or in day-to-day life (Simon, 1976, p. 8), as follows.

Synanon Game Norms	*Synanon Floor Norms*
1. Make your life public.	
2. Everyone is wrong about everything all the time in the Game.	You are either right or wrong, depending on the facts of a matter.

3. Speak the utmost syllable of your conviction.

Generally, temper conversation to keep it mannerly and civilized.

4. Polarize on all issues so the two poles are as clear as day and night.

The ability to discriminate is the ability to see the world in other than black and white terms.

5. Seek out personal confrontations. When you go into a Game, you should set out to go to war.

Generally, be friendly, courteous, and respectful of others' positions.

6. Act out!

Act as if! Even if you don't feel kindly or happy, act as if you do, and save your other feelings to "dump" them in a Game.

7. Talk about your feelings, irrational or not, in the Game.

Save highly emotional, irrational feelings for the Game.

8. Feel free to use whatever language you need to express yourself in the Game.

No foul or abusive language on the floor.

9. Say whatever you need to without fear of repercussion. The Game is a sanctuary.

Leave the Game in the Game. Action is not to be taken, generally, on the basis of information that emerges in the Game.

10. Express whatever dissent or opposition you like in the Game to anyone, even the Chairman of the Board, in whatever language you like.

Do what you are told by members appointed to positions of responsibility in the community. Save your complaints or opposition for the Game.

11. Leadership emerges of the moment in the Game. Vested authority outside the Game does not carry into the Game.

The leadership structure is established, with individuals occupying ongoing positions.

12. There is no such thing as a Game without humor. The Game should be an experience in hilarity.

Synanon Floor Norms	*Synanon Game Norms*
13. Challenge the group and what it thinks is good and bad. Conformity and consistency are the hobgoblins of little minds.	Be part of the group's efforts. Cooperation is better than competition.
14. The Game is a Game. There are no real stakes.	Life is as it is. You take your chances with your action.
15. Anything can be examined in the Game, including concepts of what the Game and Game norms should be.	
16. Randomness.	Order.
17. Undisciplined catharsis.	Dignified conduct.
18. Irreverence.	
19. Break your contracts in the Game, with friends, business associates, and spouses. Let the wind blow through your relationships.	Form your contracts. You need them to lubricate social intercourse.
20. Be as hostile as you like.	Save your hostility for the Game.
21. Defy authority.	Obey authority.

The Game is a forum for ideas to percolate, for consensus to be built, and for dissent to be expressed. It is a feedback mechanism. And it is a vehicle for the mobilizing of support, the establishment of orthodoxy, and a device for the institution of sanctions. The weekly Game is "both the glue which holds the community together and the lubricant which keeps it moving" (Newmark and Newmark, 1976, p. 96).

Synanon emphasizes health promotion rather than disease cure. The focus is on creating a healthy environment—no drugs or drinking, no smoking, daily exercise, nutritionally sound diets, and maintaining reasonable weight. Here, as elsewhere, the power of this total community exerts itself. While members are not required to eat all of their meals at Synanon, it is expected that they will do so. This expectation is reinforced by the fact that most residents lack private resources.*

* Those who come in as addicts usually have no resources. Squares

Health is so important at Synanon that an experiment is underway in the development of Health Observation Groups (HOGs). Here six to eight persons become resources for each other in the area of health. They become knowledgable as a group about their own bodies, their physical conditions, and their health habits. They formulate health-related goals and hold each other accountable for achieving them.

Although he is speaking of Synanon, what Antze has to say concerning the role of its ideology also applies to the other total community programs for addicts. The intricate demands of the Floor (as opposed to the Game) serve a number of important functions. "From the point of view of the addict, their [the demands of the Floor] greatest value may lie in their power to redirect attention. . . . the addict is likely to be someone closely attuned to his own level of stress and quite out of touch with his social environment. The Floor calls for a reversal of these habits. Unpleasant feelings are 'garbage,' and only behavior matters. What is more, activity on the Floor is so tightly structured and requires such close attention to detail that there are few opportunities to brood upon inner states. Thus, the Floor teaches a strong experiential lesson: Stress can be mastered by a simple process of ignoring it, doing one's job and 'acting as if' all were well" (Antze, 1976, p. 341).

The Game, on the other hand, presents a device for purging tensions. It is a device contrived to generate cathartic experiences. It gives the addict a way to gain relief and a way both to enjoy the pleasure of that relief as well as of the new warmth and closeness of the group. "The Game, in fact, is an arrangement that allows a player to relieve his private tensions only in an act of opening him-

---

(resident nonaddicts) often turn over most or all of their resources to Synanon. Those who live at Synanon but work outside are expected to pay a monthly fee, and there is some pressure to turn over all outside earnings. As necessary, persons are provided with "walking around money," but going outside is discouraged both by bringing to Synanon a wide array of resources and by group pressure. Recently, it has been decided that ten selected persons within Synanon will be paid salaries, from a high of $150,000 to Dederich down to $10,000 a year for others. This is described both as rewarding those who serve Synanon, and as giving them, over time, a way to amass the means to leave should they wish, the argument being that those who then stay will be the more devoted. Of course, the pay, which is all net income, as all costs of living are provided, also is a hefty carrot to keep people there. (This information is derived from personal interviews at Synanon, August 1976.)

self to others. This arrangement has an interesting consequence. Whenever a player reveals some new truth about himself, he is also forging certain emotional bonds with those who hear him. . . . the result is that a player emerges from an effective Game not only feeling refreshed and relaxed but also feeling a new closeness to his fellow players" (Antze, 1976, p. 343).

Even more than the "Anonymous" groups, Synanon's organized communities have found continuing roles for oldtimers. The emphasis is on continued involvement, which provides not only successful role models for newcomers but also continuing reinforcement for the oldtimers (Cherkas, 1965). Those who leave, however, present a bigger problem for Synanon. And, as some 90 percent of the nearly 20,000 people who entered Synanon over its nearly two decades have now left, what to make of leavers is a serious problem. At first, "Graduation" or "Third Stage" was a longed-for goal. However, the failure of some graduates to live "clean" lives, and the consequent bad publicity for Synanon, led to a period when all leavers were viewed as deserters from the Synanon way and as personal failures. As Synanon moved from a program to rehabilitate addicts (the period from 1958 to 1968) to the admission of "squares" or nonaddicts and "life-stylers," leaving took on the quality of deserting the new society. More recently, this attitude has shifted a bit; while not welcomed, or even accepted fully, it is at least recognized that some may leave Synanon and go on to successful and productive lives. Yet leaving is hard: one sixteen-year resident, who could not face the trauma of telling anyone he was leaving, just drove off in a Synanon car, parked it at the Oakland, California, facility, and disappeared. Those who remain, while acknowledging the possibility of another leaving for a positive reason, find it difficult to imagine their own leaving.

Synanon now views itself as a "secular religion," where, of course, ongoing participation is appropriate. Current developments reflect this view. "Currently, the Synanon life-style has been adopted by approximately 1,400 live-in residents, the majority exaddicts, with a significant and growing contingent of non-character-disordered individuals. Synanon's primary base of operations is a 3,000-acre ranch complex in Marin County, California. On this collection of properties a 'Synanon City' is being built. Seven hundred fifty people reside there, where Synanon operates its own school system, rehabilitation programs and varied business enterprises. With construction teams having built over fifty new living structures over the past few years, this Synanon II community represents the first significant step in Synanon's utopian March out of the world of dreams into the process of building an alternative social order" (Simon, 1976, p. 4). If this description seems overblown, that is in part because Simon is a "true believer," but also because Synanon's ambitions are grand. Although Synanon is more than a mutual aid group, as such, it represents, in an extreme form, some of the positive and negative aspects of such groups.

Synanon brings many positives to the lives of its residents. These include an active and dynamic life; being a part of a larger whole; a sense of shared values and commitment; a kind of openness and honesty; heterogeneity of age, race, class, and backgrounds among its members;* and an integrated community. It offers these benefits, of course, at some cost, primarily to what most would call the *value of individualism*. What for some is a sense of shared purpose can also be experienced as a unified ideology. What for some is an integrated community can also be seen as an overcontrolled life. And what for some is allegiance to a higher power (or leader) can also be viewed as subservience. These issues enter into hot debates about the value of Synanon in particular and about self-help mutual aid groups in general.

Although AA's founder, Bill W., is much revered, the role of Dederich is of even greater centrality to Synanon. In part, of course, this is a function of Synanon's smaller size and greater geographic cohesiveness. But it is also a function of how Dederich behaves—in a recent interview he said, "I am not concerned about my authority. There has never been any questioning of it" (Wilkins, 1976, p. 87)—and of how Synanon is organized: Its top leadership includes Dederich's present wife and the two children of his former marriages, one of whom (Jady) is the heir apparent. Dederich's

* Sexism, however, does exist at Synanon. For example, when the "square" men shaved their heads in support of the addicts, who are shorn as part of the "cold turkey" process, "square" women were prohibited from doing so. Only later did one woman shave her head; she was then followed by the others.

role goes beyond the Synanon centers themselves. For example, Daytop Village, a New York City drug program, was established in 1963 after its founders paid a visit to Dederich's Santa Monica center. (Indeed, many present-day drug programs are extensions of Synanon, either programatically or because they are led by former residents of Synanon.)

Daytop Village. Daytop rejects treating the addict as a sick person needing medical treatment, as a criminal needing jail, or as a victim needing sympathy. Rather, according to the Daytop philosophy, the "addict is an adult acting like a baby: childishly immature, full of demands, empty of offerings" (Bassin, 1968, p. 48). In essence, the addict is seen as a psychopathic personality, always taking, unable to give. The addict, according to Daytop's philosophy, refuses to take responsibility for his or her actions or to recognize that the fault is his or hers. Taking the posture that the addict is both a reluctant enrollee (therapy and change being viewed as only the lesser evil, compared with jail or continuing on the street) and a "con artist," Daytop's initial posture is both standoffish and questioning. The addict must prove his or her desire to be in the program, and must do so in the face of severe questioning from the oldtimers. For the moment, the addict must *behave* as if he or she were responsible, "must *act as if* you understand, *act as if* you are a man [sic], *act as if* you want to do the right thing, *act as if* you care about other people, *act as if* you are a mature human being" (Bassin, 1968, p. 51—emphasis in original). The addict is asked to play a new role without requiring that he or she necessarily understand it. This focus on learning how to behave in a new role without requiring that the person necessarily understand it characterizes all of the self-help groups described in this chapter. Indeed, role theory is a central explanatory factor in understanding the effect of self-help groups. (See Chapter Four for a discussion of this and other factors.)

Modeled on Synanon's Game, the thrice-weekly encounter session is Daytop's key group-therapeutic technique. David Dietch, Daytop's director (and a Synanon graduate) describes the encounter as "a gut-level teaching device that speeds up personality alteration, just as a pressure cooker speeds up the preparation of food" (Bassin, 1968, p. 52). Speaking of the decision to expand Daytop Village from its initial group of thirty males, Dietch says, "The junkie needs new faces on whom to try out his recently acquired skills. It is necessary to create a community of men, women and children who live and work and love together if our people are to grow into mature responsible citizens."

While the newcomers provide "objects" on whom the old-timers can try out their newly acquired skills (a good illustration of the "helper-therapy" principle), the oldtimers also provide peer models for the newer members. Participants are supposed to be responsible both for their own behavior and for that of the other members of the group. In this total living situation, the peer-based method "powerfully reinforces more adaptive behavior" (Vattano, 1972, p. 10).

Delancey Street. Another offshoot of Synanon is San Francisco's Delancey Street (Hampden-Turner, 1976), founded in 1968 by John Maher, a drug user who found the constraints of Synanon too binding. "Maher incorporated those concepts that had worked for Synanon: no drugs or violence, the game, the need to locate in rich neighborhoods, a return to the early American work ethic to end the individual's dependence on welfare, federal grants, corporate and foundation funds. He rejected the ideas of Synanon that he felt were proven failures: Synanon had withdrawn to an isolated, utopian community that had no contact with current social movements. . . . Synanon took no part in politics; Delancey Street's political clubs would get out the vote for supportive candidates and would lobby to change laws. Synanon discouraged its people from leaving the commune to live and work on the outside; Delancey Street would aim to put the exaddict back with society as a productive member with strong economic and emotional ties to the community" (Sales, 1976, p. 60).

The Palo Alto Veterans Administration Group. Also borrowing heavily from Synanon is a "peer confrontation" program at Palo Alto Veterans Administration Hospital (Van Stone and Gilbert, 1972). The participants are male inpatients on an open psychiatric ward "seeking help with alcoholism, drug dependence, gambling, sexual deviation, repeated conflicts with the law, and other self-defeating life-styles" (Van Stone and Gilbert, 1972, p. 583). The key characteristics of the program are "An individualized negotiated treatment contract between each potential participant

member and his peers; a twenty-four-hour-a-day live-in setting . . .
a supportive drug- and medication-free environment oriented toward
personal growth and learning; a highly authoritarian, member-con-
trolled social structure constantly evolving from within the membership; and periodic group confrontation sessions with strict rules
including energetic verbal confrontation of each member regarding
self-destructive behavior admixed with warmth and empathy of a
'super-family.' These five characterstics, working together, appear
specifically to counteract and contain severe authority conflicts, dependency, underlying hostility, and profound narcissism with certain
patients classified as having character defects" (Van Stone and
Gilbert, 1972, p. 587)'.

Recovery, Inc., and Other Expatient Groups

The groups described in this chapter on self-help in mental
health can be thought of as aligned along a continuum. (Actually,
a broad-band spectrum may be a more appropriate metaphor, in
that there are a group of characteristics around which we can
cluster the groups, but for now let us look at the continuum.) The
groups at one end—AA and the other "Anonymous" groups, Synanon, and Daytop—see their participants as persons with chronic
conditions who have hit bottom and are incapable of helping themselves. The activities of the program, whether or not the program is
residential, become central to the participants, and "the way" of the
group is viewed as the only solution for the individual. These groups
are entirely led by lay people (except for Daytop, which was founded
by professionals). The groups that we will discuss later in this chapter, such as the national Parents Without Partners, have participants
whose conditions are not chronic (although they may continue for
a long period) and who are not viewed (nor do they view themselves) as having hit bottom or being helpless (although, of course,
they need help). Further, while these latter groups are important to
their members, they are not the locus of the individual's life, nor
do they have a formal philosophy and exegesis that are to be
religiously followed. Professionals are often involved on an ongoing
basis, and there is no glorification of a leader or founder.

Recovery, Inc., and the other groups we will discuss in this section fall somewhere in the middle between these two sets of groups. Described by its executive director as "a lay-run self-help, after-care, group meeting organization designed by a Chicago psychiatrist to prevent relapses in former mental patients and chronic symptoms in nervous patients" (Borman, 1975, p. 53), Recovery views its members as in need of long-term participation but recognizes that one can eventually get better. The group is important to its members, but it is not residential, as are Synanon and Daytop, nor are meetings as frequent as those of AA. If the participants have "hit bottom," that level of the problem has already been dealt with while the individual was hospitalized. Thus, when participants arrive at Recovery they are capable of helping themselves. In addition, two studies, made a decade apart, found that prior to entering the group about half of Recovery's members had not been hospitalized, and a quarter had not had any psychiatric treatment (Wechsler, 1960a; Grosz, 1972). There is a Recovery "way," a text, and a revered leader, not all of which features apply to the other expatient groups. Moreover, Recovery, unlike some of the other expatient groups, was professionally founded and sees itself as an adjunct to professional care.

Recovery is the largest of the expatient groups—a 1973 study reported 850 Recovery groups with 15,000 members, All other expatient organizations combined were reported to have fewer than 400 groups and less than 3,000 members (Gussow and Tracy, 1973).* In 1975, the executive director of Recovery reported 1,045 groups in the United States, Canada, and Puerto Rico (Borman, 1975, p. 53).

Founded in 1937 by Chicago psychiatrist Abraham A. Low, Recovery was "designed to encourage his patients to carry out a self-help program that would permit them to control their symptoms" (Lee, 1976, p. 43). It operates on the principle that, while patients returning from psychiatric hospitals are greatly improved, they still have "residual symptoms" (Lee, 1976, p. 43). Low de-

---

* This dominance of the field by Recovery has been true for the past twenty years. A 1957 study by the Joint Commission on Mental Illness and Health reported approximately 5,000 members in 42 organizations of mental patients, with an estimated 4,000 of them in the then 250 Recovery groups (Wechsler, 1960b, p. 50).

scribed the returning patients as "mostly afraid of . . . terrifying sensations, threatening impulses, obsessing thoughts and depressing feelings, that is, their own inner experience" (Low, 1950, p. 18).

In sharp contrast to the groups described earlier, Recovery members' working relationships with professionals were a central feature from the outset. And, although Recovery had nearly 700 groups, no article on Recovery appeared in any professional journal until 1971 (Park, 1976, p. 408). However, since 1969, a session on Recovery has regularly been included in the convention program of the American Psychiatric Association, and in 1975 the Psychiatry Specialty Boards Examinations included a question about Recovery.

Like the other groups, Recovery's weekly meetings are rigidly structured. They begin with an introduction of members by their first names (as in AA), followed by readings from Low's book *Mental Health Through Will Training* (1950). (Some Recovery groups use recordings of Low's comments, akin to the AA and GA readings of their "Twelve Steps" and Synanon's use of tapes by Dederich.) Then members present examples of their behavior and "spot" on the examples. The central Recovery technique of "spotting" requires that members identify particular aspects of their thinking and behavior according to Recovery's concepts for maintaining mental health. (This is similar to AA's personal testimonials and GA's "weather reports," but there is no formal group interaction to match Synanon's Game.) Unlike the other groups described, Recovery meetings close with a request for donations of money, and questions from newcomers are answered. Group socializing is not encouraged nor is extensive out-of-meeting contact, as Recovery prefers members to interact within the confines (and control) of the group.

In addition to "spotting" on behavior, Recovery participants are trained in "self-endorsement" (Lee, 1976). Members are told they must endorse themselves (give themselves praise) every time they make the effort to use Recovery methods. Although "spotting" and "self-endorsement" are methods to be used outside of the group, the Recovery participant learns them and tries them out in the group setting. Such discussions are conducted using a special Recovery language, with psychiatric terms forbidden. The reason for this is explained as to keep inexperienced people from straying into areas about which they are ignorant, "but it also serves to keep the group's attention on those things they can do to exercise the self-help concept" (Lee, 1976, p. 44). Of course, it also serves to build the sense of the group as special, with its own unique language.

Like the other self-help groups, Recovery focuses on specifics of behavior. Members are told to "command your muscles." Insomnia is to be overcome by commanding your muscles to lie quietly; jealously to be countered by commanding your muscles not to rummage through your husband's pockets or wife's mail" (Low, 1950, p. 310). "The muscles can reeducate the brain," as Low puts it, or, in language nearly identical with that used at Synanon, "If the member acts normal for a long period of time, he will begin to feel normal, too" (Antze, 1976, p. 335).

By providing understanding and support, the group serves as an instrument for combatting loneliness and isolation felt by the expatient. In addition, the Recovery group provides an advantageous element of competition: "Patients consciously or unconsciously compete with one another to see who can improve most completely and quickly and thereby win the approval of the rest of the group. In turn, the actual demonstration of objective improvement from week to week is a source of great encouragement and inspiration to the others. Part of the program for each is the support and reclamation of other patients. The spirit of working together toward a common goal cannot be overemphasized. In union there is strength. Helping others is one of the surest ways to help one's self. These truths have been known through the ages. In Recovery they are brought into sharp focus where patients can actually observe them in practice" (Dean, 1971, p. 76).

This mix of both cooperativeness and competition is not the only dualism in the Recovery design. There is also the tension between whether the patients can truly get better or whether they will always continue in the expatient role. Further, there is the question of the extent to which the patients' efforts are self-sufficient or whether Low's dicta are the essential factor. Recovery's official brochure states that "The Recovery method consists of (1) studying Dr. Low's book *Mental Health Through Will Training* and other literature, plus records and tapes recorded by Dr. Low; (2) regular attendance at Recovery meetings; and (3) the practice of Recovery principles in one's daily life" (*Recovery*, 1973, p. 3).

Another important aspect of Recovery, in addition to the

group's role and Recovery's "way," is how it delegates the leadership function. "Groups are led by former patients who have been members for six months or longer of Recovery, who have been trained in the regular Recovery meetings and at monthly area leader meetings and who are authorized from year to year as group leaders" (Borman, 1975, p. 53)'.

The leaders are responsible for two things: to lead the weekly meetings (unlike AA and GA, where leadership rotates among the lay members), and, as Recovery's Executive Director Robert Farwell states, "to follow the proscription that we do not advise, consult, diagnose, or treat" (Borman, 1975, p. 54). As he puts it, "It is lay run. We deal in what we refer to as trivialities. We do not, if possible, interfere with but rather cooperate with medical and psychiatric and other counseling that a person may be getting simultaneously or before" (Borman, 1975, p. 54).

While Recovery's "ideal referral comes from a physician or psychiatrist" (Dean, 1971, p. 77), if the need arises it will accept members who, for economic or other reasons, are not currently under psychiatric care. In response to certain professional objections to this procedure, Stanley Dean makes the following comment: "Does that [acceptance of patients not presently under psychiatric care] pose a threat to private practice? Not at all. The present author can affirm that a physician who refers selected patients to Recovery will find that it is like bread cast upon the waters—in terms of cross-referrals, therapeutic progress, prestige, and self-esteem" (Dean, 1971, p. 77). This is a far cry from AA's aggressive assertion that nobody makes money from AA. However, at least one report finds Recovery to be much like AA, calling it "a kind of cult, with highly ritualized and formalized behavior, with a charismatic leader who expounds the Word, and with a dogma and exegesis" (Landy and Singer, 1961, p. 31)'.

Three studies—one a sampling of the entire Recovery membership in 1961 (Wechsler, 1961), another based on data collected about 6,463 members attending 500 Recovery groups in 1970, at which date there were 784 Recovery groups (Grosz, 1973), and the third a study of a single program operated by Camarillo State Hospital (California) reported on in 1971 (Lee, 1976)—give some idea of the characteristics of Recovery members. (Unfortunately, the data collected in each study are not easily comparable.) The first study, comparing members to the population of their home communities, found them to be of a fairly high socioeconomic level (according to education, occupation, and family income); similar in religious affiliation; more likely to be married; slightly younger than average; and disproportionately female (Wechsler, 1961). The two later studies confirmed the preponderance of females but offered mixed evidence as to the levels of education and age (Lee, 1976; Grosz, 1973). Also, the 1971 study found the number of nonwhites (race was not studied in the two earlier studies) to be disproportionately low (Grosz, 1973).

The 1970 study of 500 Recovery groups found that 44 percent of the groups had ten or fewer members (5 percent had more than twenty-six); 56 percent of the members were forty-one years of age or older; and 73 percent were female. The largest occupational group, 47 percent, were housewives, and 64 percent of the members' families had incomes of $10,000 or less. Nearly half (48 percent) had not been hospitalized prior to entering Recovery, and 30 percent had not been treated for a nervous or mental condition before joining Recovery (Grosz, 1973).

The Camarillo State Hospital study also looked at the illness characteristics of the participants. In the Recovery group, compared with the hospital's overall population, there was an overrepresentation of schizophrenics and people with psychotic depressions and depressive reactions, and an underrepresentation of patients with chronic brain syndrome and personality disorder diagnoses (Lee, 1976).

The 1961 study looked at Recovery not as a variety of self-help but as a type of voluntary community organization. The author found that "the members of this specialized group showed many of the personal characteristics attributed to members of voluntary community organizations" (Wechsler, 1961). He concluded that

The members of the self-help organization were found to differ from other residents in their home communities in a number of ways which would be expected to exist between joiners and the general population. In addition, despite the fact that the members were either former mental patients or persons who were encountering psychiatric difficulties, they were found to be relatively active in other voluntary community organizations besides the self-help group. A comparison of the self-help organization members who were inactive, moderately active, and very active revealed the same type of relationships between extent of participation and selected personal characteristics that had been obtained in general studies of voluntary community organizations. [Wechsler, 1961, p. 622]

Wechsler's study is unique in the field; perhaps because it was pathbreaking it is also limited—it does not compare Recovery's members to those of voluntary community organizations nor does it consider the nature of the involvement and participation of the Recovery members in other organizations. However, Wechsler's study makes clear that one of the facets of the self-help organization that requires more attention is its group function. We will examine that feature more closely in Chapter Four.

Emphasis on the role of the group is also found in Mowrer's Integrity Groups concept (Mowrer, 1971a, 1971b, 1974; Mowrer and Vattano, 1974, 1976). Responding to the growing sense of alienation as traditional primary groups weaken, Mowrer, a psychologist, sees "the new small group movement [as representing] an attempt to create, not just a kind of 'therapy,' but actually a *new primary social group*, or institution, which will compensate for these basic human losses" (Mowrer, 1971c, p. 45—emphasis in the original).

Founded in 1961, the Integrity Groups grew out of Mowrer's efforts to find a way to establish warmer relationships with clients in his clinical practice. Indeed, one of the unique features of Integrity Groups is that professionals are involved as equal members rather than as leaders or therapists. "Special responsibilities, such as Group Chairman or Council Representative, revolve, and the obligation to give as well as receive help is widely diffused. Every therapist is also a patient (if one wishes to use these terms), every student a teacher" (Mowrer, 1971c, p. 48). However, Mowrer does see a special role for professionals in starting nonprofessional mutual aid groups; indeed, he has run graduate seminars at the University of Illinois to train such persons (Mowrer, 1971c, pp. 48–49). Mowrer distinguishes between the AA-type peer group, in which all the persons have the same problem and there is no status distinction, and the Integrity Group peer group, which includes persons of diverse background who are "equals, without status or rank, except as special functions may be temporarily assigned to them—or in terms of informally recognized group experience or competence" (Mowrer, 1971c, p. 49). Thus, while the professional may also give as well as get, he or she does have a special role to play in Integrity Groups. Unlike Recovery, however, Mowrer emphasizes that the very nature of the group prohibits a fee relationship: "Since Integrity Groups are dedicated to the principle and practice of *mutual* help, it is assumed that membership and participation in such groups will not involve a fee or charge of any kind" (Mowrer and Vattano, 1976, p. 425—emphasis in the original).

Mowrer also suggests a broadening of the self-help concept to emphasize mutual aid, "which implies give and take." This combination of self-reliance and mutual support is expressed in the Integrity Group's motto, "We alone can do it, but we cannot do it alone" (Mowrer, 1971c, p. 49).

Mowrer goes so far as to propose that "everyone ought to be in a mutual aid or peer group (for the bearing and sharing of 'one another's burdens') not as 'therapy' but as a *way of life*" (Mowrer, 1971c, p. 53—emphasis in the original). The characteristics of such groups would no doubt closely resemble the present Integrity Groups, which have the following features:

1. A well-defined structure.
2. Goals that focus on each member's responsibility for changing himself.
3. Group intake, with modeling procedures demonstrated by experienced members.
4. A contractual agreement to embrace the core values of honesty, responsibility, and involvement.
5. A commitment to move beyond self-disclosure by translating words into deeds.
6. Leadership shared by participants.

Integrity Groups have a decalog of commitments that members pledge to honor. A member agrees that, both in and out of

Integrity Groups, he or she will not do the following (Mowrer and Vattano, 1976, p. 76).

1. Won't interrupt.
2. Won't blame.
3. Won't "act off" negative emotions.
4. Won't "sub-group" [form factions or cliques].
5. Won't "yes, but" [retain reservations].
6. Won't "talk back or argue."
7. Won't mind-read [decide what someone else is thinking]—or expect others to do so.
8. Won't cheat.
9. Won't double-talk [say one thing and mean another].
10. Won't tit-for-tat [respond to negative behavior with equally negative behavior].

Through the self-disclosure and feedback techniques that are common to other mutual aid groups—but also through introspection, which is not—Integrity group members become aware of specific aspects of their behavior that are personally and interpersonally dysfunctional. "Once an individual has indicated the areas he wishes to deal with, the Group helps him pinpoint specific environmental or interpersonal experiences where he can test out new ways of behaving" (Mowrer and Vattano, 1976, p. 429). Individuals are expected then to make a commitment of specific intention to carry out some action. At one point, Integrity Groups even kept "commitment books," in which individual members recorded their commitments. The group then "becomes an *internalized reinforcer* for individual behavior change. This is the most important element in accounting for how an individual's verbal commitment results in his ability to exercise 'self-control' over his behavior" (Mowrer and Vattano, 1976, p. 430—emphasis in the original).

While not properly labeled an expatient group, Neurotics Anonymous (NA) does include many expatients; indeed, its founder, Grover, was both an alcoholic and undergoing psychiatric treatment. NA follows "the AA Recovery Program as adapted for neurotics" (*Neurotics Anonymous,* 1966, p. 3). As such, NA, while not hostile toward the professional mental health community, can be best described as distanced from it.

There are a considerable number and wide variety of other expatient groups. Some (20 percent, according to a 1957 survey) are run entirely by participants (Wechsler, 1961), such as a club for former patients at Massachusetts Mental Health Center (Landy and Singer, 1961), while others are run by professionals (Wechsler, 1961; Lurie and Ron, 1971). Some, such as the Massachusetts Group, provide simply a place for expatients to gather, while others, following Recovery, offer "therapeutic" activities. In England, professional-led follow-up groups for discharged patients are part of an integrated mental health service system (Katz, 1965); some sixty groups are organized as part of Depressives Associated, with headquarters in Dorset.

"Halfway houses" and some "day hospitals" also have self-help characteristics. A notable case is the "Lodge Program" (Sanders, 1976), organized by a California state mental hospital, where male patients who were ready to be discharged volunteered to live in a building in the community and organized a janitorial business (and later a gardening service), which they managed and conducted as they did the affairs of the lodge. Professional services were not provided by the hospital, although a rarely used veto power was held over decisions. "Compared to their matched control, a significantly greater proportion of the individuals in the lodge situation were able to remain out of the hospital and to assume employment" (Sanders, 1976, p. 182).

The obverse of Wechsler's point that those who join Recovery are much like joiners of other community voluntary organizations, of course, is that those who are less likely to be joiners in general will be less likely to join an expatient group. In addition, there is the stigma still associated with mental illness and patients' desire to forget about their hospitalization (Palmer, 1968). Joining such a group means, in effect, accepting the expatient role and thus differentiating oneself from the general community. Many may wish to "pass" as a nonexpatient (Wechsler, 1961). Moreover, the absence of clear termination procedures (and the implication of the person's condition being chronic, as seems to be the case with Recovery) may lead to continued dependency. It is possible that Mowrer's notion of everyone participating in a mutual aid group might serve to destigmatize it. On the other hand, just as Parsons has described "socialization into the patient role" (Parsons, 1951), so these groups may socialize expatients into a well role (Lee, 1971).

"Living With" Groups

All of the groups we have described thus far deal with people who, depending on one's classification system and prior assumptions, are sick, or patients, or seem to be inadequate in some way. The groups to be described here (and in the next section, "people alone") do not fit into these categories. While these group members have problems, these problems are not their own but those of someone with whom they live—spouse, child, or parent.

Where the problem is that of an adult, auxiliary groups for spouses (for example, Al-Anon and Gam-Anon) and children (Alateen and Prison Children Anonymous) have been established, or spouses are welcomed to at least some of the activities of the self-help group itself (Gamblers Anonymous, Recovery, Mended Hearts, Prison Families Anonymous, and Huntington's Disease). Essentially, the thrust of these efforts is to inform the relative of the nature of the problem faced by his or her family member and to aid the relative both in coping with the problem and providing understanding and support to the afflicted person.

When the afflicted person is a child, the family members, particularly parents, are required to play a more active role. Gussow and Tracy (1973) have grouped self-help organizations into two categories: Type I includes those that provide "direct services to individuals and relatives in the form of education, skills, encouragement, and other forms of support," while Type II organizations are "more foundation-oriented, promoting research, fund-raising, public and professional education and legislative and lobbying activities" (Gussow and Tracy, 1973). Caplan, however, notes that "by campaigning politically for improvement of the community's handling of the needs of people like themselves," the members of Type II organizations are in fact developing "cohesion and some sense of mastery over cruel fate" (Caplan, 1974, p. 23). In other words, the activities of what Gussow and Tracy call Type II organizations have Type I effects on the participants. The range of such groups covers nearly all of the afflictions from which children can suffer. In Massachusetts alone, for example, there are groups for parents of twins and multiple births; of retarded children; of emotionally disturbed, physically handicapped children; of children who face hospitalization, leukemia, cystic fibrosis, congenital heart disorders, Down's Syndrome, rubella, spina bifida, Tay-Sachs, cleft palate and/or lip, cerebral palsy, hemophilia, brain injury; and of those who are blind or deaf; as well as a group for parents whose child has died (*A Directory of Mutual Help Organizations in Massachusetts,* 1974).

The specific activities of the individual group vary, of course, depending on the nature of the child's affliction, but the general functions and activities are quite similar. Some were organized as a service activity of a large organization (United Cerebral Palsy), and others were organized by the parents themselves (particularly those related to retarded children). Many were organized by hospitals either as part of their program or as a response to parents' desires to get together with persons like themselves. Other groups simply grew out of parents being together in a waiting room of a special clinic serving their children!

Examples of two groups serve to illustrate this type of self-help activity. The first example deals with parents who learn at their child's birth (or soon thereafter) that the child has Down's Syndrome; the second with parents whose children are dying of leukemia.

For parents of children with Down's Syndrome (and other, similar diseases), what had been anticipated as a joyful occasion, namely birth, becomes the opposite. The medical staff often handle their own disappointment by suggesting institutionalization, by exhortations to the parents to love the child, or by avoiding the parents. The parents, for their part, often react with an unwillingness to develop attachments to the child; friends and relatives are encouraged not to visit (or do not on their own); and birth announcements are not made. The parents lack knowledge of what the child will look like, what he or she can do and will need to have done for him or her. And since they probably do not know anyone else with such a child, their grief is compounded by isolation (Murphy, Penschel, and Schneider, 1973).

At group meetings, new members tell how they learned about their child's illness and how they responded, while old members tell of their own experiences and changes over time. Members practice (role play) how to tell others and how to respond to them. Information is shared on how to deal with children on a day-to-day basis, what to expect and what to do. "The group mitigates feelings of isolation and depression. Members could see how other children appeared and acted. The discovery that other parents had similar feelings and fears reassured them of their own adequacy and sanity. Some parents served as role models to illustrate that it is possible to survive such an event" (Murphy, Penschel, and Schneider, 1973, p. 119).

For parents of children with cystic fibrosis, the group performs a similar set of functions. "The group meeting provided a sounding board for parents to learn, to devise, to consider, and to test new methods of coping as well as to receive reinforcement for prior satisfactory adjustments. Parents repeatedly expressed a sense of comfort in learning that their grief, pain and everyday difficulties were not unlike those of others" (Driscoll and Lubin, 1972, p. 146).

Parents of children with leukemia go through a process of anticipatory mourning following stages not unlike those of parents of children with Down's Syndrome: first denial, including "shopping around" for alternative diagnoses, then anger, bargaining, depression, and finally acceptance (Knapp and Hansen, 1973). Groups for such parents deal with issues such as disciplinary problems with the patient and siblings' and peers' reactions to physical changes in the patient, the patient's own questions and fears, the relationships between the parents and their child (or children).

In evaluating the experience of the group, parents have emphasized the value of realizing that they were not alone; that there was a place where they could express their actual feelings (for example, at times not wanting to be with the child or being angry with him or her for being ill) without feeling guilty; and that they could anticipate and learn how to deal with problems and try out solutions. For some parents, the group became the vehicle that enabled them to talk to each other about their child's illness (Knapp and Hansen, 1973, p. 74).

Talking about their feelings with someone who has been there is an overwhelming need for parents whose young children have died, particularly those who are victims of Sudden Infant Death Syndrome (SIDS), formerly called "crib death." As one mother said, "Whenever I get it on my mind and I can't seem to function, I call someone in the Foundation (for Sudden Infant Death). 'Am I nuts? Am I going crazy?' It's comforting to hear her say 'No, I've been through this too. Everybody gets these feelings. It's part of the natural grieving process' " (Steinmann, 1976, p. 41). Founded in 1962 by a Connecticut couple whose baby died, the Foundation now has forty-three chapters, while the International Council for Infant Survival, started in 1964 by a couple whose two-month-old daughter died, has twenty-three affiliates.

With parents of children whose problem is serious but not life threatening, a different set of activities takes place. For example, the Greater Omaha Association for Retarded Citizens not only organizes groups of parents of retarded children but within the groups, parents new to the group are paired with long-time members to provide emotional support from someone who has "already been there," facts about mental retardation, information about services available, tips about ways to arrange things, and introductions to other parents of retarded children (Katz, 1975a). In Yugoslavia, a program for physicially handicapped children involves parents in discussion groups about the children and their problems, as well as engaging them in helping with the children's therapy (Katz, 1975b). This is similar to the various programs in which parents learn to provide early stimulation for their retarded children.

Although not precisely a self-help activity as we have been using the concept, it is worth noting the increasing number of programs that train parents as therapists to work with their own children (Guerney, 1964; Schloper and Loftin, 1969; Schloper and Reichler, 1971; Wahler, 1969). The Kendall Center (in Chapel Hill, North Carolina) incorporates into its program of training parents as therapists a parents' mutual-help group where they are able to share both their experiences as parents of retarded children and as therapists in training. Of particular value is the opportunity for "older" parents to report to the newer parents on changes in their children as a result of their own role as therapists (Stabler, Gibson, and Cutting, 1973).

Life Transition Groups

Discussing various types of mutual aid community support groups, Caplan distinguishes between those organizations designed to help their members break a harmful habit, such as alcoholism, drug abuse, smoking, or overeating and others that emphasize the formation of a new community in which members undergoing role transitions can immerse themselves. Falling into the second category are parent groups such as those we have just discussed; "people alone" groups, including widows' associations; adolescent and older persons' groups; Parents Without Partners; and women in the process of becoming mothers. "The association with others in the same situation combats the social isolation that would otherwise be the lot of those who feel themselves, and are perceived by others, to be deviant in ordinary society" (Caplan, 1974, pp. 21–22). (Of course, the last group, pregnant women, although it does share with the others the involvement in a transition, does not share the sense of deviance that characterizes the others.)

Both the parent and "people alone" groups not only provide emotional and social support "but they usually provide detailed information and specific guidance in increasing their members' understanding of the issues involved in their predicament and of practical ways of dealing with the expectable day-to-day and long-term problems" (Caplan, 1974, p. 23).

Parents Without Partners. Founded in 1957, Parents Without Partners (PWP) is the largest group of single parents, with more than 200 chapters and some 30,000 members, about three quarters of whom are women (Katz and Bender, 1976, p. 69; Egelson and Egelson, 1961; Weiss, 1973). Unlike the "Anonymous" and expatient groups, membership in PWP is subject to considerable turnover: During its first ten years, over 100,000 persons were members at one time or another (Gould, 1968).

Weiss makes a point similar to that made by Caplan, noting that for some PWP members "the organization was responsive to the marital loss itself" and for others it was "responsive to the defects of life as a single parent" (Weiss, 1973, p. 332). For the first group, more likely divorced (or separated) than widowed, the organization met individuals' needs "to be able to talk to understanding and sympathetic listeners about their feelings, their concerns, and their plans" (Weiss, 1973, p. 332). For the second group, already having made the transition from marriage to life on their own, PWP met their "relational deficits, [that is], distressing absences of important relational provisions." Weiss points to four "continuing sources of stress" to which PWP responds: (1) the absence of a sustaining community; (2) the absence of similarly placed friends; (3) the absence of support for a sense of worth; and (4) the absence of emotional attachment (Weiss, 1973, p. 332; Weiss, 1969). The leaders of PWP play down the charge that PWP is simply a dating service, both because they wish to avoid the pejorative implications of that charge (and its attendant loss of attraction of "nice people") and because they see their work as having broader scope, as indeed it does.

This broader scope, however, expressed in the characterization of PWP by a professional adviser to its national headquarters as "an educational therapeutic advisory organization" (Gould, 1968, p. 666), presupposes an initial acceptance of the stigma of an inferior position; the belief is that " 'parents *with* partners'—in keeping with the prevailing social norm—are better" (Katz, 1965, p. 70). Indeed, PWP's recognition of this stigma may be seen in the current discussion within PWP to change its name to "Single Parents, International." An additional stigma is faced by divorced Catholics, given their doctrinal belief that a valid marriage is indissoluble in the eyes of God. It is no surprise, then, that more than 150 groups of formerly married Catholics have sprung up in the past five years. Most have 100 to 150 members; one (Nassau County, New York) has over 700 members. Many of the groups are part of the new North American Conference of Separated and Divorced Catholics, although each club is autonomous.

Yet another set of problems face young, unmarried, black mothers. While sharing many problems with white women, with whom they participated in a self-help group called "The Mamas," three years ago a group of New York City black women organized the "Sisterhood of Black Single Mothers" because they felt the problems faced by single black women were more fundamental, often related to basic questions of survival. One of the main goals of the Sisterhood is to remove the stigma and personal shame of being a single mother. In addition, members provide both an emotional support network and concrete services (exchange of clothes and furnishings, babysitting, cash in emergencies) for each other.

La Leche League. New mothers share the process of role transition with Parents Without Partners. La Leche League (LLL), organized in 1956 by a group of women in the Chicago area to share their experiences with nursing babies, has since expanded its scope to broader issues of mothering. There are now some 1,000 groups, part of a centrally controlled organization.

The formal La Leche activity is a series of four structured meetings. Participants include pregnant women, new mothers, as well as mothers with several children. Often, persons stay with a group and thus help others by sharing their experiences. It is this "having been there" factor that is central. As one member said, "La Leche League is more accepting of a mother's feelings than any doctor or any other person can be. They really understand how hard it is to be stuck with a crying baby. They don't make you feel guilty, or as if you're supposed to be a saint" (Silverman and Murrow, 1976, p. 413). And in the words of another, "After the baby was born, I was so exhausted and discouraged, and I thought it would last forever. The women in LLL helped me to understand that the baby and I were in a temporary period of adjustment, and that it would pass" (Silverman and Murrow, 1976, p. 414).

Those who are parents of twins are faced with the same exhaustion and discouragement but without the comfort of the sense that their situation is temporary. In 1934, the National Twins Association was established "to promote the spiritual, intellectual, and social welfare of twins throughout the world" (Babagian, 1976–1977, p. 5; the name was changed to the International Twins Association in 1937). At present, there are 6,767 members in 185 clubs located in forty states.

*Widow Groups.** As we have noted, the nature of the group

* It is not sexist to call these "widow" programs. Not only are women more likely to lose a spouse due to death (5.9 per 1,000 for men versus

can be seen in the way the problem is identified. As those in Parents Without Partners may feel themselves inferior to those with partners, so, too, often the widowed feel inferior to the nonwidowed. "Many women see widowhood as a social stigma. They see themselves as marked women, different from everyone else, even carrying this so far as seeing themselves as defective, that something must be wrong with them if they lost their husbands" (Silverman, 1970, pp. 545–546). This sense of stigma, felt by many of those involved in the groups we have discussed, can be mitigated by the help of someone with the same condition. The stigmatized individual needs to feel that "he [or she] is human and essentially normal in spite of appearances and in spite of his own self-doubts. . . . The first set of sympathetic others is, of course, those who share his stigma. Knowing from their own experience what it is like to have this particular stigma, some of them can provide the individual with instructions in the tricks of the trade and with a circle of lament to which he can withdraw for normal support and for the comfort of feeling at home, at ease, accepted as a person who really is like any other normal person" (Goffman, 1963, p. 83).

This is exactly the function played by the widow aide in the Widow-to-Widow program established in 1967 by the Laboratory of Community Psychiatry at Harvard Medical School (Silverman, 1970). Both the formal auspices of this program and the use of a paid worker (who, in addition, shares widowhood with those served) make this program different from the pure self-help groups. However, the activities of the program are fully in the mode of the self-help groups we have discussed earlier. The program was begun as an experiment in preventing emotional problems in a bereaved group. "It was hypothesized that if another widow reached out to the new widow, she would be accepted as a friend because she was someone who understood since she had been there herself" (Silverman, 1970, p. 543). As one widow put it, "Since you are a widow too, when you said you understand I knew you meant it and that was so important. I can't stand sympathy and that's all anyone else could give me" (Silverman, 1970, p. 545).

13.9 for women), and to live longer in a state of widowhood (an average of 18.5 years for women and 13.5 years for men), but women also participate disproportionately in such programs (Silverman, 1972).

While there are group meetings, most of the work of the Harvard program is done through one-to-one contacts between widow aides and the widowed. Here, "the aide is using her own experience as a human being and as a widow to guide her encounter with the new widow; she appreciates the real need that exists but she never takes the widow's initiative away from her" (Silverman, 1970, pp. 542–543). More recently, a telephone hotline service, the Widow Service Line, has been developed. It is staffed by volunteers who have been helped by the Widow-to-Widow program and supervised by two of the initial widow aides (Abrahams, 1972). Beyond providing aid in coping with the trauma of becoming a widow—and, as Silverman points out, this upset is not eased by an institutionalized rite of passage the way engagement eases the transition to marriage—the widow aides help the widows adapt to the widow role, which means accepting that the spouse is dead and that new life patterns must be developed. The widow must now learn to make decisions without help and guidance from a husband, to learn to be alone, and to recognize and act on the need to make new friends and to be out among people (Silverman, 1970, p. 544). The widow aides, using their own experience, help the widows both to face the fact of widowhood and then to learn how to manage their own lives.

Although not as carefully organized as the Harvard program, there are many programs for widows that involve other widows as caregivers and that recognize the benefit gained by the caregiver as well (Abrahams, 1976). The extent of these programs is not surprising, given the large numbers of widowed persons—10 million in 1970, 85 percent of whom were women (Silverman, 1972, p. 95). Such groups often sprout up quite independently. Some programs focus on crisis intervention by therapists, while others are oriented more toward self-help; all see in the experience of the widowed a resource for helping others with the same experience.

Groups for Older People. Similarly, the Senior Companions program of ACTION builds on the experience of one older person in the help he or she gives to another. While here the participants share being old, in the other two ACTION programs involving older persons as givers of service, Foster Grandparents and SERVE, the members help, respectively, children and persons of all ages (Bowles, 1976).

According to national evaluation studies of the three programs, the two top-ranked, self-perceived benefits to volunteers are "feelings of usefulness and importance" and "increased satisfaction with life" (Booz, Allen, and Hamilton, 1975; E. F. Shelley and Co., 1973; Booz and Allen Public Administration Services, Inc., 1975). In addition to their role vis-à-vis those with whom they work, in all three programs participants have established support systems with each other, coming together both formally, for inservice training, and informally. Since most live alone, this support is especially meaningful. In discussing SERVE (Serve and Enrich Retirement by Volunteer Experience), which provided the model for RSVP (Resources to Serve in Volunteer Programs), SERVE's founder notes that the "group provided the volunteers with peer support in the work setting and with the social contact and opportunities for friendship which so many older persons need" (Sainer, 1976, p. 75). These benefits seem to be characteristic of each of the programs.

In an insightful analysis, Hess points out that in the concepts of support systems and self-help are "two of the most enduring themes of sociology, the quest for community, and the ability of human groups to adapt the conditions of existence through the creation of social role structures" (Hess, 1976b, p. 55). In part, the need for the creation of these new structures is a function of both the longer lives people lead and the growing percentage of the population that is older. Not only are people living longer, but they are also retiring earlier; the combination means a longer period of postretirement life. For example, between 1900 and 1970, there was a 10 percent drop in the percentage of their life adult males spent in the work force (Johnston, 1972). And not only do the current group of older people have (on the average) a decade or so of postretirement life, they "must do so without clearly established rules or guides to appropriate behavior and without new roles of commensurate value in our society" (Hess, 1976b, p. 55). In this context, mutual support and self-help groups are less to be wondered at than expected.

As we note later, in the discussion of youth, in age-related groups it is difficult to draw a sharp line both between informal activities and organized groups, as well as between spontaneous groups and those organized by professional service givers. While groups of this last type may lack some of the aprofessional character of AA and similar efforts, they nonetheless incorporate many of the other basic characteristics of self-help mutual aid. In age-segregated communities, helping relationships most often evolve out of daily interaction. For example, at Merrill Court, a small apartment building that houses lower-middle-class widows in the San Francisco Bay Area, an informal self-help pattern has developed (Hochschild, 1973). The women, from sixty to eighty years of age, live in their own apartments, but engage in a variety of group activities, many involving mutual aid. Both the absence of customary support systems and characteristics shared by the residents (sex, age, family status, class, and history—most are from the rural Midwest) encourage the establishment of "an alternative to the nuclear family" (Hochschild, 1973, p. 50). A similar pattern of relationships is described as having developed at a mobile home community for retired working-class people (Johnson, 1971).

Less spontaneous are those efforts organized by a social service worker or other outsider. At a low-income inner-city trailer park, a mental health aide organized the elderly into a rather complex surrogate kinship network providing material and emotional support and a mechanism for collective problem solving (Hess, 1976b, p. 60). Hess summarizes such circumstances, stating that "Under conditions of normlessness and loss of customary role interaction, old people are likely to devise spontaneous helping patterns which frequently mirror those of extended families. In some cases, the intervention of social workers or managers may be needed either to initiate the interaction or to provide continuity through time" (Hess, 1976b, p. 60).

A quite unique example of mutual aid among older persons is the Senior Circle in Synanon. We have noted already the central role of its founder, Dederich; his role in shaping the attitudes toward and the expectations from older persons is also central. He has said, "There is no such thing as a dying person. Either you are living or you are dead" (Newmark and Newmark, 1976, p. 94). This attitude suggests the belief that older persons can lead full and exciting lives until the day they die; indeed, at Synanon it is expected that they will do so and will contribute to the life of the community. At present, there are at Synanon about thirty people, sixty to eighty-five years of age, the formerly character disordered as well as former "squares." Most of these people live at the Santa Monica facility, where the Senior Circle members (earlier they had called themselves the "Mummies" and then the "Old Farts") have their own apartments, work and recreate side-by-side with the younger members.

Synanon seeks to balance the assistance giving to members who need it—the two men who bathe and shave a partially disabled resident—with emphasis on those capabilities a person still has and making the most of them; the same disabled man works in Synanon's direct mail business. Change is constant at Synanon. To some extent, planned change is a way for the community to remain active. New activities spread fast and wide through Synanon. And, so, too, it is assumed that old people can change. For example, while the skills of a man who for thirty years prior to coming to Synanon had been a baker were used in the kitchen, after he had trained a group of younger members he was encouraged to learn new skills and to hold jobs other than that of baker.

Youth. It is not surprising that self-help mutual aid activities have developed rapidly among youth in the past decade. Not only do youth have problems that the traditional care-giving systems have not been able to meet, but the structure of these systems, as well as the larger society of which they are a reflection, also present youth with special problems. Fundamentally, youth are given little opportunity to do, to contribute, and to grow. Mutual aid self-help activities give youth a chance to do just that, to make a positive contribution to others, as well as to benefit themselves. Just as with older persons who are extruded from the work force, youth, who are blocked from entering it (in part, of course, because there are too few jobs), find in mutual aid activities both something useful to do and something that is of personal benefit.

Perhaps more so than in the other areas of our concern, it is difficult to delimit those activities concerning youth that fall within our present focus. This is in part because the involvement of youth in mutual aid activities is of a piece with central features of adolescence—the grouping together, sharing of values and feelings, and pattern of conformity to the groups' norms. To some extent, therefore, one can think of peer mutual aid group activities as a formalizing of these features.

Several sets of activities involve youth in activities that partake of some of the dimensions of mutual aid. In peer counseling, one youth counsels another (Brown, 1974; Delworth, 1974; Eberly, 1977; Hamberg and Varenhorst, 1972; Zunker and Brown, 1966), with emphasis on the benefit to the counselee, while in peer cocounseling it is the reciprocal relationship that is central—that is, the benefit is seen as mutual for the counselor and counselee (Dollar, 1976). Similarly, in youth-tutoring-youth and children's learning-through-teaching programs there is the sense of benefit for both the tutor and student (Allen, 1976; Gartner, Kohler, and Riessman, 1971; Lippitt, Eiseman, and Lippitt, 1969; Newmark, 1976; Thelen, 1967).

From another perspective, the result of playing the tutor role is similar to the result of "as if" roles mentioned earlier in this chapter. That is, the child "placed in the tutor role . . . discovers that he must live up to its expectations" (Allen, 1976, p. 21). In other words, the child tutor comes to behave "as if" he or she were seriously committed to learning, and thus actually becomes committed. And for children from whom little has been asked, to be placed in a nurturant role, "to take responsibility for another person . . . may foster more socially mature behavior in general" (Allen, 1976, p. 22).

While cocounseling goes beyond peer counseling, just as learning-by-teaching goes beyond simple tutoring, basically both are one-to-one activities. In peer cocounseling and learning-by-teaching programs, the group context is added. While some learning-by-teaching programs include groups (for example, a school in Pacoima, California, and the schoolwide learning-by-teaching demonstration being developed at Public School 133 in Central Harlem), it is primarily in other types of youth programs that the full mutual aid design is operative—in programs such as walk-in counseling centers, rap rooms, runaway houses, free clinics, halfway houses, and therapeutic communities (Glasscote, 1975), as well as, on occasion, in youth treatment hospital programs (Johnson and Peebles, 1973).

While the special situation of a hospital places certain constraints on the program, a different set of circumstances obtain in a school-based program. The Rap Room at Woodlands High School (in Hartsdale, New York) is a drop-in mutual counseling effort, made possible by the interaction among the students and a very active psychologist who is both leader and trainer as well as participant.

As with other groups, Rap Room has its own language, customs, and rules. It has developed as an institution both within and alongside of the high school. As its founder notes, "Probably the most serious problem has been the lack of incorporation and utilization of Rap Room and its cadre into the school mainstream" (Petrillo, 1976, p. 57). Yet, when some "bad" pills (capsule drugs) had been unloaded on the high school, it was the Rap Room students who were concerned, skilled, and trusted by their peers enough to round up the pills. And some fifty of the Rap Room group have conducted a workshop for school district administrative staff, as well as conducting "Magic Circle" groups for seventh-grade students.

Something of the flavor of the Rap Room, especially the interaction among the youth and the role of the psychologist, is illustrated in the following description by Pearlman (1976, pp. 11–13).

At the beginning of a session, a young woman looked around the room and asked "Where's Amy? I just found out she's been cutting History for the past two months. I thought she had changed that class, she'd been gone so long. But yesterday, the teacher announced she's in real trouble." Others had seen her around the building and knew this was the period she regularly attended rap and that she was probably copping out. Although rap is voluntary and is a revolving door, the group felt that Amy would really want to be called on her behavior. Several offered to go find her. It was decided that if she strongly protested she wouldn't have to come back but that she would be encouraged to. When her friends returned with Amy, she was asked about her cutting, her not asking for help, her denial (the way in which she didn't acknowledge that she was failing). A number of people expressed concern; a few others were indignant that she had vocally and energetically confronted others without exposing the skeleton in her closet. A dramatic moment ensued when one very articulate young man, Jim, pulled his own covers by facing Amy squarely and saying, "I can't believe you; you're throwing away your education. All you have to do is go to that class and you can pass. I can't read. I can go to that class everyday and get a tutor and still not necessarily pass and you have it easy and still don't do it. I can't believe you. *Why?*" Amy started crying. She let go of her previous answers ("I don't like the class," "I get hungry at that time," and so on) and finally turned to Jane, saying, "You're the reason I don't go. I know it sounds silly but since you really started snubbing me it has been too painful to go to that class." The room grew more gentle and carefully helped Amy and Jane explore their friendship. (It was beautiful and unusual to observe the respect everyone expressed towards a friendship in trouble. It was also extremely moving to see Amy break through the image of bravado, which many adolescents seldom disturb, to expose her own deep vulnerability at being rejected.) The confrontation moved to its final productive rebuilding stage and contracts were made to help Amy catch up on the classwork. This incident ran into the next period so that many people had slipped out. However, Jane remained to hug Amy on the way out and the leader said, "Although Jim has left, I want you all to be aware that he sent Amy a real love letter. He has never exposed his reading problem and today he did so in order to help Amy. Let's show him some concern the next time he comes in." He turned to Amy and asked her where she would be studying Saturday night. She said she'd be babysitting. "Will you give me a call to let me know how it's going? I'd really like to hear from you." and he handed her his home phone number. She smiled saying, "I don't know why I didn't do this sooner." The leader replied, "You're doing it now and that's what counts."

This incident illustrates much about Rap Room, and similar mutual aid peer groups. It is active and confronting, real experiences are used, and appropriate behavior is modeled by peers. The technology involved includes self-disclosure, self-exploration, self-growth, and the positive use of catharsis. The professional participates, providing both advice and modeling behavior.

Less structured than Rap Room is Hotline, an alternative

service program in a suburban community outside of Washington, D.C. (Gordon, 1976). At one level, Hotline is a place where the young people found other people who were like them. " 'When I came to 'Hotline,' one phone aide told me, 'I first realized that there were other people in the world that were sensitive, and had the blues and stuff' " (Gordon, 1976, p. 50). But it was not identity alone, it was helping and being helped. "As they spoke with young people their own age they learned about themselves. They drew on their own experience—hassles with school or parents; bummers on drugs; fears of sex or abandonment—to 'relate to' the callers, and came to value it more. In urging anonymous young people to 'face situations' and 'confront' parents, and 'seek out resources,' they were reminding themselves to do the same" (Gordon, 1976, p. 51).

As an organic community, Hotline had to struggle with the relationships between its (adult) founder and the newly acquired strength of the youth. In keeping with the ethos of Hotline, a monthly group was organized where both the counselors and the leaders could share their concerns. A culmination of this came when the founder was able to share with the group problems she was having with her children and to seek its help: "The 'second mother' became a friend and comrade" (Gordon, 1976, p. 53). Increasingly, the youth who participated most fully in Hotline began to take responsibility for it, to recruit and train new counselors, and, in doing so, began learning for themselves. Thus not only were Hotline's services a form of "helper-therapy" (Riessman, 1965), but the very operation of it was as well.

Summary

Perhaps the single most important common denominator of the various types of self-help groups we have looked at in this chapter is that the role of the person who has already lived through the experience is critical for helping others. Not only does that person know what it is like, but he or she has also learned how to play the required new role—the alcoholic who has stopped drinking, the mental patient who is now well, or the person whose spouse has died and now accepts the state of widowhood.

While the groups share in the importance of the role of the

person who has already lived through the experience, they differ in a number of ways. We have already noted Caplan's distinction between the groups designed to help their members break a noxious habit (such as AA, Gamblers Anonymous, and Synanon) and those for persons who are undergoing a role transition and for whom the groups provide a new community (Parents Without Partners, the widow groups, La Leche League, and the youth groups).

A central difference relates to the role and involvement of professionals. AA and those groups closest to it are totally lay run. They are neither organized nor led by professionals. On the other hand, the groups of parents of children with particular illnesses generally have been organized by professionals and often are led by them. Some of the newer groups, such as Parents Anonymous and Prison Families Anonymous, combine a central role for laypersons with professional backup. In Chapter Five, we will examine in detail the issue of professional relationships to self-help groups, but first we will turn to self-help in health.

3

Emerging Forms of Self-Help Health Care

★★★★★★★★★★★★★★★★★

In advanced technological society, the major health problems are not those of acute illness, in which the doctor plays a crucial, curative role, but rather those of chronic illness, in which the patient plays the strategic role. In the last fifty years, the incidence of infectious illness has been reduced, largely as a result of improved food, sanitation, and housing. But in the longer lives that people live, they are subject, instead, to a broad range of chronic disorders, such as diabetes, mental illness, cancer, heart disorder, hypertension, arthritis, and emphysema. About 50 percent of the population now suffers from chronic illnesses, and these disorders account for 70 percent of all doctor visits (Gerson and Strauss, 1975).

Strauss (1973) described some necessary steps that can enable chronic illness sufferers to cope with their illness. Three dimensions are critical for the chronically disabled patient:

1. The ability to read signs that portend a crisis; for example, a diabetic's ability to recognize the signs of oncoming sugar shortage or insulin shock or an epileptic's ability to recognize an oncoming convulsion. In a sense, this ability is a form of self-diagnosis.
2. The ability to respond to the crisis of the moment; for example, diabetics may carry sugar or candy or insulin and epileptics may stuff handkerchiefs between their teeth just before convulsions. These are, in a sense, forms of self-treatment.
3. The ability to establish and maintain a regimen. The extent to which a person is able to do this depends on his or her belief in the efficacy of the regimen.

All three of these abilities are central characteristics of a consumer-centered model of health care. For these steps to be carried out, for the patient indeed to be a producer of his or her own health, he or she must be trained in matters traditionally the prerogative of the professional, must be encouraged to be an active participant in the achievement of the cure, must be "turned on" to doing so, and must be convinced of the efficacy of the undertaking (Strauss, 1973, p. 36).

The involvement of laypersons in health care is a wide-ranging practice, and has diverse origins. One study (Green, Werlin, and Schauffler, 1976, p. 27) notes that "Such factors as the movement toward consumer participation in government programs and community development, the self-directed behavior and behavior modification movement, the evolution of nursing theory and practice from 'helping the helpless' toward facilitating self-care, and the evolution of group dynamics and self-help groups have all contributed to this trend."

This trend is occurring within the framework of serious fiscal constraints in our economy and considerable criticism of the nature and organization of professional care regarding quality, efficiency, and cost. Thus these activities are a part of a broader trend toward involving consumers in the fulfillment of their own needs. Many of these activities derive their power from the concept adumbrated by Victor Fuchs (1968), that in the services the consumer is a producer. While we would give greater weight to the importance of structual changes than does Fuchs, particularly those related to broad environmental conditions, physical as well as social (note in this regard the findings of Brenner [1976] regarding the correlation between economic factors such as unemployment and suicides, mental institution commitments, and infant mortality), we agree with Fuchs (1974, p. 151) as to the importance of individual consumer behavior: "By changing institutions and creating new programs, we can make medical care more accessible and deliver it more efficiently, but the greatest potential for improving health lies in what we do and don't do for and to ourselves."

Self-Help Health Groups: Characteristics and Growth

Self-help groups in the health field have evolved to meet the needs not only of chronic patients, but also of patients emerging from the acute phase of long-term disorders, such as strokes and heart attacks. Organizations such as Mended Hearts, Reach to Recovery, the Stroke Club, and Laryngectomy, Inc. help patients adjust to their new situation after an operation or other highly specific treatment for the acute phase of their illness. The laryngectomy group helps club members perfect speech techniques. Reach for Recovery helps patients face the psychic problems associated with mastectomy (breast loss), along with interpersonal, marital, and sexual problems, and their fear that the cancer may recur. These services are often consumer initiated and play an enormous role in the rehabilitative process; indeed, the major health organizations are now sponsoring self-help clubs (for example, the American Cancer Society supports the laryngectomy, mastectomy, and ostomy groups, and at a recent convention the American Heart Association recommended that its state affiliates encourage and promote the establishment of stroke clubs).

The groups just mentioned are for people who themselves have a problem. Other groups are for people whose spouses, parents, or children have a problem. We have already noted Al-Anon, for the spouses of AA members; Alateen, for their children; and other such groups, in our discussion of mental health groups. More elaborate are the groups for parents of children who have some illness. The largest are the lobbying organizations of parents of handicapped children, which have brought about, by bringing suits, some of the major breakthroughs in education and care for these children. We have already illustrated the range of such groups by listing the organizations of this type operating in Massachusetts. The range of these groups can also be seen in the following listing of self-help groups in health care, classified according to World Health Organization disease categories (from Gussow and Tracy, 1973).

Addiction
>   Addicts Anonymous
>   Al-Anon
>   Alateen
>   Calix Society
>   Gam-Anon
>   Gamblers Anonymous
>   Synanon Foundation

Blood Conditions
>   Candlelighters (cancer)
>   Cooley's Anemia Blood and Research Foundation for
>   Children
>   National Rare Blood Club

Bronchopulmonary Conditions
>   Black Lung Association
>   Emphysema Anonymous

Endocrine Conditions
>   Human Growth, Inc.

Health Maintenance Groups
>   Anti-Coronary Club
>   Medic-Alert Foundation International
>   Saved by the Belt Club

Intelligence
>   Association for Advancement of Blind Children
>   Association for Children with Learning Disabilities
>   Association for Children with Retarded Mental Development

Association for the Help of Retarded Children
Mongoloid Development Council
Mothers of Young Mongoloids
National Association for Gifted Children
National Association for Retarded Children
New York Association for Brain-Injured Children
Orton Society
Retarded Infants Services

Infant Mortality
National Foundation for Sudden Infant Death

Mental Illness
American Schizophrenia Association
Mental Patients Liberation Project
Mental Patients Political Action Committee
Mental Patients Resistance
Mothers Anonymous (Parents Anonymous)
National Society for Autistic Children
Neurotics Anonymous International Liaison
Radical Therapists
Recovery, Inc.
Schizophrenic Anonymous International
The Bridge, Inc.

Neuromuscular Disorders
California Association for Neurologically Handicapped
    Children
Committee to Combat Huntington's Disease
Dyautonomia Association
Louisiana Epilepsy Association
Myasthenia Gravis Foundation
National Tay-Sachs and Allied Disease Association
Stroke Club

Obesity
Buxom Belle, International
Fatties Anonymous
TOPS (Take Off Pounds Sensibly)
Overeaters Anonymous
Weight Watchers, International, Inc.

Physical Disabilities
> American Wheelchair Bowling Association
> Disabled Officers Association
> National Amputation Foundation
> National Association of the Physically Handicapped
> National Wheelchair Athletic Association
> Paralyzed Veterans of America

Sensory Disorders
> American Federation of Catholic Workers for the Blind
> Association for Education of the Visually Handicapped
> Athletics for the Blind
> Blinded Veterans Association
> Choose, Inc.
> International Parents Organization
> Myopia International Research Foundation
> National Association of the Deaf
> National Federation of the Blind
> National Fraternal Society
> National Industries for the Blind
> Retinitis Pigmentosa Foundation

Skin Disorders
> Leanon Chapter
> Psoriasis Research Foundation

Surgeries
> International Association of Laryngectomees
> Mended Hearts
> Reach to Recovery
> Society for the Rehabilitation of the Facially Disfigured
> United Ostomy Association

One of the most important expressions of self-help in the health field, of course, is found in the feminist perspective. Marieskind and Ehrenreich (1975, p. 36) give the following overview:

Today there are approximately 1,200 groups in the United States which identify themselves as part of the women's health movement, and tens of thousands of women who consider themselves to be participants in this movement. In addition, there are women's health groups and projects throughout Europe and in Canada, New Zealand, Australia, and South America. Perhaps the best indication of the movement's growing self-consciousness is the existence of two national publications, both devoted to intramovement communication and debate. *The Monthly Extract: An Irregular Periodical* has been in existence since August 1972, and *HealthRight* since late 1974. The movement has produced a large and distinctive body of literature, including books (*Our Bodies, Ourselves* by the Boston Women's Health Collective [1972] of which 750,000 copies have been sold).

As noted in our discussion of mental health groups (see Chapter Two), Gussow and Tracy (1973) have developed a two-dimensional analysis of self-help groups in the health field. Type I groups provide direct services to patients and their relatives in the form of mutual assistance, encouragement, education, skills, and support in efforts at helping them deal effectively and adaptively with the focal conditions. Such groups can be truly called *mutual help health organizations*. They include such organizations as Emphysema Anonymous, Mended Hearts, Stroke Club, the ostomy clubs, groups related to the various addictive conditions (abuse of alcohol and other drugs, gambling, and overweight), and, as noted in Chapter Two, a large number of mental illness organizations. Type II organizations place more emphasis on promoting research, fund raising, public and professional education campaigns, and conducting legislative and lobbying activities.

The two types of groups are not always mutually exclusive. Sometimes the classification of a group is only a matter of degree; Type I groups are also concerned about research and education of professionals, and some Type II groups do provide indirect services.

Despite a wide diversity in etiology, symptomatology, and disease course, Type I clubs tend to form around conditions for which there is no medical cure beyond that for acute phases (this alone may account for the fact that the major infectious diseases are not represented by any self-help group), where there is a residue of chronic impairment, where problematic medical, social and psychological effects remain, and where survival beyond the acute phase entails disability. Further, and perhaps most important, these are conditions for

which a viable life-style is often possible when appropriate rehabilitative procedures are followed. This last criterion is the main deter-
minant for certain medical conditions to be predisposed toward foundation-oriented organizations rather than mutual help groups. The
Committee to Combat Huntington's Disease (Huntington's Chorea) is
an example. The organization was founded in 1967 by the wife of a
patient to help others cope with the course and outcome of the disease.
Mutual support, however, soon became a secondary function, as no
amount of help and encouragement could retard the progress of the
disease, and for the patient the potential of a future viable life-style is
nil. Benefits lay not in following a regimen of rehabilitation but in increasing basic scientific research. The committee shifted from a Type
I to a Type II organization early in its career. [Gussow and Tracy,
1973, p. 3]

   We propose dividing the Gussow and Tracy Type I self-help
groups into four categories. Groups in the first category are engaged
in *rehabilitative work*. Here the doctor has already dealt with the
patients in the acute phase, and the self-help activities are concerned with helping the patients adjust to their new situation. Interaction with others who have undergone similar experiences provides a body of special inside information about the stages of
recovery and how to function; coping techniques; role models; an
emotional outlet; and support and encouragement. Groups such as
Mastectomy, Inc., Mended Hearts, Stroke Club, United Ostomy
Association, International Association of Laryngectomees, and the
Fraternity of the Wooden Leg; the several groups for those who
have had kidney transplants or are undergoing renal dialysis; and
the new groups of those with cancer, such as Make Today Count,
are examples of groups engaged in rehabilitative work.
   A second type of mutual aid group is concerned with the
behavior change of those engaged in activities such as drug abuse,
overeating, and smoking. Among these groups are Alcoholics
Anonymous, Weight Watchers, TOPS, and Smokenders.
   A third type includes groups that engage in *primary care*.
They largely operate in the area of chronic care, where there is no
cure but where care is necessary. These self-help groups provide
important assistance to patients in adjusting their life-style and incorporate social processes into the dynamics of coping and adjust-

ing. Such groups include Emphysema Anonymous, the Arthritis Federation, and the American Diabetes Association. Another example in the area of primary care is women's health groups, often operating out of the feminist health centers that provide direct care for women. These groups emphasize the common experiences of women, the special nature of women's health concerns, and the development of a shared ethos.

A fourth, less developed, type of self-help activity is in the area of *prevention* and *case finding*. An example is in the field of hypertension. Here there are two activities. One is primary care activity, where self-help techniques can be applied to encouraging and supporting people in the regimen of taking prescribed drugs, weight reduction, and exercise. The other activity is based on the role participation in such a group can play in preventing heart attacks, kidney disorders, and so forth. A combination of prevention and case finding operates in the Health Observation Groups being developed at Synanon, where small groups of members engage in mutual observation and monitoring of each other's health, as well as in providing informal care and a forum for discussion of health issues.

Although the range of self-help groups encompasses the entire spectrum of health issues, including persons with illnesses in which death is likely (see the discussion, later in this chapter, regarding groups among kidney transplants and those with cancer), "most functioning members of self-help health groups are not *in extremis*. The disease process therefore is not the overriding consideration" (Tracy and Gussow, 1976, p. 387). The groups deal primarily with the adaptive problems of the participants. At a personal level, this includes dealing with problems of uncertainty, body image, and emotional support. At the social level, there are problems of interaction with family members, friends, work colleagues, medical personnel, and with the public at large, as well as broader issues of stigmatization.

Self-Help Groups in the Health Field: Selected Examples

While interest in self-help health groups has heightened in the recent period, many of them are not new—the International

Laryngectomee Association was founded in 1942, the Anti-Coronary Club in 1957, Mended Hearts in 1951, Reach to Recovery in 1952, and TOPS in 1948. Table 2 shows the size of some of the largest self-help health groups, as well as date of formation.

Table 2. The larger self-help health groups.

Name	Number of Clubs/Chapters	Members	Date Founded
Emphysema Anonymous	7	2,000	1965
International Association of Laryngectomees	233	NA[a]	1952
Mended Hearts	42	4,200	1951
Myasthenia Gravis	33	20,000	1952
National Foundation for Ileitis and Colitis	14	8,000	1965
Overeaters Anonymous	474	NA[a]	1960
Paralyzed Veterans	27	7,500	1945
Stroke Club	80	3,000	1968
TOPS	12,000	300,000	1948
United Ostomy Association	400	25,000	1962
Weight Watchers	NA[a]	2,000,000	1962

[a] NA—data not available.
Source: Data on International Association of Laryngectomees, "The International Association of Laryngectomees Directory, 1976." Data on TOPS, "News from TOPS" (1975). Data on United Ostomy of America, "United Ostomy Association, Inc." (1975). All other data, Gussow and Tracy (1973).

Rehabilitation. The focus of the groups concerned with rehabilitation, which fall into our first category, is the nature of the individual's condition and the problems of rehabilitation and adjusting to it. To the society at large, the clubs (and their national organizations) provide information, particularly emphasizing the ability of the individual to return to his or her prior life—to work, recreation, family roles, and sexual relations. To the individual, the clubs (but not Reach to Recovery, which is essentially a one-to-one activity) provide models of success, information about and training in coping techniques (as well as information about necessary devices for the ostomate and laryngectomee), advice to spouses, and a forum to practice new or relearned behaviors, as well as encouragement and support.

As Tracy and Gussow (1976) point out, the medical condition of most of the participants in self-help groups is not acute. Pointing to the high morbidity and mortality among kidney transplant patients—within three years following transplantation, over 58 percent will lose their graft and 39 percent will die (Advisory Committee to Renal Transplant Registry, 1975)—Kleeman and De Pree (1976) suggest this as a factor accounting for such patients' low participation levels in self-help groups. Kleeman and De Pree (1976, p. 73) conclude that "those with relatively stable medical careers are more likely to become members than those with more volatile physical conditions." However, although the volatility of the illness appears to be an important factor as to the extent of a person's participation in self-help group activities, it is interesting to note that self-help groups are now developing among cancer patients (Pellman, 1976; Robertson, 1976). This development seems to be a function of the increasing "cure" rates for cancer patients,* of a greater desire for openness and honesty, as well as of a growing acceptance of the efficacy of the self-help modality itself. The first example of a rehabilitation group we will discuss is Make Today Count, which is exclusively for cancer patients. Of the remaining three examples, the first two—the United Ostomy Association and the International Association of Laryngectomees—maintain close links with the American Cancer Society, as the conditions with which they deal are frequently related to cancer.

Make Today Count. Make Today Count has some 3,500 members in seventy chapters. It was organized in Burlington, Iowa, in 1974, following a newspaper story by Orville Kelly, who has lymphoma, calling for an organization of persons with "incurable" diseases. Make Today Count includes cancer patients, their families, and medical personnel. Although professionals are involved as members and some chapters have local professional organizations as sponsors (the Monroe County Cancer and Leukemia Association in Rochester, New York, for example), Make Today Count is less professionally dominated than the International Association of

---

* In the 1930s, one person in five with diagnosed cancer was still alive after five years; the figure in the 1970s is one person in three.

Laryngectomees. On the other hand, Kelly is now the head of a National Cancer Institute program in Iowa to coordinate services for cancer patients. Emphasizing the "care" feature that characterizes all self-help groups, Kelly says he has learned to "live with cancer, not die from it" (Pellman, 1976, p. 44).

United Ostomy Association (UOA). "Like Mastectomy, Ostomy Surgery Needs More Public Exposure," reads the headline of a press release issued by the United Ostomy Association, Inc. There are approximately 110,000 ostomies annually (including colostomies, which account for 65 percent of the total; iliostomies, 25 percent, and urostomies, 10 percent), compared with 90,000 mastectomies; some one and a half million persons in North America have had ostomies. UOA's Executive Director, Donald P. Binder, in noting that "many famous people are ostomates," expresses the hope that "Someday, one of them will do for ostomy surgery what Mrs. Betty Ford, Mrs. Nelson Rockefeller, Mrs. Shirley Temple Black, and Mrs. Marvella Bayh have done for mastectomy" (*Like Mastectomy,* undated p. 2).

Informing the public at large and ostomates in particular about ostomies is a major activity of UOA. The first ostomy group was formed in 1949, when a Philadelphia doctor encouraged five ostomates to meet and share their knowledge and experience of ostomy. ("The word *ostomy* signifies a type of surgery required when a person has lost the normal function of the bowel or bladder. . . . The ostomy allows normal body wastes to be expelled through a surgical opening (stoma) on the abdominal wall" ["UOA," 1975, p. 2]). The ostomy clubs developed rapidly in the 1950s, within a few years after ileostomy operations began to be performed regularly (Lennenberg and Rowbotham, 1970). Local associations spread, and in 1962 a national organization was formed with twenty-eight chapters. A decade later, there were 170 chapters; and another four years later there were nearly 400 local affiliated ostomy chapters in the United States and Canada (the sudden spurt of growth being due to improved surgical procedures). In 1974, the International Ostomy Association was organized, with nine national member associations.

The kinds of basic information UOA presents are illustrated

by a brief brochure, "So You Have—Or Will Have an Ostomy" (1975, pp. 3–6), which answers questions such as the following:

1. Why haven't you met any ostomates?
2. But how can YOU adjust to living without a normal rectum or bladder opening?
3. Will you bulge?
4. Will you smell?
5. Will you make noises?
6. Will you feel the waste discharges?
7. Will you be a captive of the toilet?
8. Will you be a social outcast?
9. Will you get/stay married? Have babies?
10. Will you easily bathe, go swimming? Bend over?

The essential answer to all of these questions is that "Once ostomates have been rehabilitated, they can look forward to normal productive lives. Ostomy surgery need not limit one's capacity to live an active life" ("United Ostomy Association," 1975, p. 4).

Local chapters provide one-to-one help for new ostomates and mutual aid and moral support among their members. Most meet monthly and have educational programs and group discussions. Nationally, UOA publishes a journal, Ostomy Quarterly, as well as a range of other publications, including guides to the three types of ostomies, special publications for professionals, two publications about child ostomates (one to explain a child's ostomy to him/her and the other for the parents of an ostomate child), and three publications on sexual aspects (for single ostomates; about pregnancy; and for male ostomates).

International Association of Laryngectomees (IAL). While UOA chapters maintain links with local Cancer Society groups, the American Cancer Society (ACS) "sponsors the IAL, its National Office, and its programs, financially" (Laryngectomized Speakers' Source Book, 1975, p. 28). IAL was founded in 1952 when thirteen clubs, the first formed in 1942, came together at a conference sponsored by the American Cancer Society; the U.S. Department of Health, Education and Welfare; and Western Reserve

University. This involvement with ACS is reflected in the volume and nature of IAL's publications, in its elaborate organizational structure (the 1976 *Directory,* includes a ten-page listing of national officers, directors, and committees), and in its close ties to organized medicine.

As with UOA, the adaptation to the new condition—here, the partial or total removel of the larynx—involves the care of the stoma, as well as the learning of esophageal speech. (Two thirds of all laryngectomees speak with esophageal voice, 10 percent with artificial devices, 5 percent through both, and 12 percent do not speak at all.) Most IAL groups (generally called Lost Chord or New Voice Clubs) provide instruction in speech, usually through a university and Cancer Society instructor. Since 1960, an annual Voice Rehabilitation Institute has been conducted (funded by the U.S. Department of Health, Education and Welfare) training both lay larynegectomized instructors and professionals to teach esophageal speech. While acknowledging the value of the "having been through the mill" experience of the laryngectomized instructors, IAL's position favors the professional speech pathologist.

"A laryngectomee can do almost anything after his operation that he did before," proclaims an IAL brochure (*Laryngectomees at Work,* 1975, p. 2). Much of what a laryngectomee can do may be influenced by the activities of local club members. They often visit patients prior to the operation, as well as after. (Access to patients is controlled by the surgeon, and IAL does not challenge this, even in instances where surgeons discharge patients without informing them of resources for learning how to speak again.) The model visitor is a well-adjusted laryngectomee, who can speak and who has a job. (About three quarters of successful laryngectomees retain their jobs [Ranney, 1975].) The clubs provide "a form of group therapy, where people sharing the same disability support each other's morale with encouragement and example of successful readjustment. The social situation, with other laryngectomees and their wives participating in normal activities, exchanging ideas and experiences, is in itself a means of reintroducing the timid and uncertain laryngectomees back to normal life" (Ranney, 1969, p. 75–S). The reference to laryngectomees and their wives in this quotation is not a case of sexism: Among the 9,000 or so new cases each year in the United States (of whom about 3,000 die), the ratio is more than eight men to one woman.

Reach to Recovery. The activities of Reach to Recovery are much like those of UOA and IAL; here, too, there has been a surgical procedure to which the patient must now adjust. Unlike the ostomate or laryngectomee, the mastectomate does not have a device whose use she must master. However, her surgeon has almost surely been a man and is rarely prepared to respond to the myriad concerns she has as a woman. The Reach to Recovery volunteer is thus frequently a key factor in her adjustment. As with IAL, Reach to Recovery is affiliated with the American Cancer Society, and the surgeon's control of access to patients is unchallenged.

The Stroke Clubs. The stroke clubs are more locally organized. Unlike laryngectomy, mastectomy, or ostomy—where the medical condition, while severe, is nonetheless limited—the recovering stroke patient, at least at first, is often relegated "to the status of non-person" (Tracy and Gussow, 1976, p. 389). Stroke patients often cannot speak and people talk as if the patients were not there, although, of course, they can hear. Training stroke patients to communicate through finger pressure is one of the ways that stroke club members can help new victims. Moreover, those stroke victims who have aphasia and whose speech pattern is often slow—which others frequently meet with impatience—frequently feel and express frustration and anger, which results in withdrawal and passivity by both the patients and those who interact with the victims. "Self-help groups are aware that under such circumstances relationships deteriorate; through their activities they alert family members to these interactional contingencies" (Tracy and Gussow, 1976, p. 389).

Behavior Change. As the most frequent individual health problem is overweight, it is not surprising that the groups concerned with it have the most members—half a million people come through Weight Watchers doors each week (Warren Adamsbaum, personal communication, 1976); TOPS (Take Off Pounds Sensibly) has 300,000 members in 12,000 chapters in 29 countries ("Fact Sheet," 1975); and a study of group dieting reports "that at least 52,000,000 Americans are calorie conscious" (Allon, 1973, p. 37). Although pervasive, the problem of overweight (except in rare cases, with which the groups do not deal) is not as serious as those that concern the rehabilitative groups or the groups that deal with such forms of addictive behavior as alcohol or drug use. (Many of the techniques used by such "addiction" groups are those of behavior change, and the decision to deal with them in Chapter Two, on mental health, and to discuss weight-related groups here, is arbitrary.)

Take Off Pounds Sensibly (TOPS). Although for some conditions around which self-help groups organize, the "problem" does much to dictate the approach and activities of the groups (for example, the ostomy and laryngectomy groups), in other cases the formulation is more open. We have noted in Chapter Two, for example, that Parents Without Partners, a name and formulation that makes a statement about what is normal (that is, parents with partners), is considering a name change, to Single Parents, Inc., which also signifies a change in their perspective. Similarly, the conceptualization of obesity is not a fixed matter. Being overweight can be understood as a physical matter, as an emotional problem, or as a function of socially determined norms of beauty.

The basic approach of the two largest groups, Weight Watchers and TOPS, is to see overweight as an emotional problem. "Emotional control is a central virtue in the TOPS philosophy, which views overeating and overweight as signs of defective control" (Stunkard, 1972, p. 146). As with AA, on which it was in part modeled, TOPS is a nonmedical group (although its founder, Esther A. Manz, a Milwaukee homemaker, did so with her doctor's encouragement) that has continued to function and grow despite rapid turnover within individual groups. One study reports that nearly 50 percent of those enrolled dropped out within six months (Wagonfeld and Wolowitz, 1968), while another notes that "TOPS serves, at the very least, as a way of selecting people who are ready to lose weight" (Stunkard, 1972, p. 143). Both studies note that among those who remain there is an impressive weight loss. Stunkard's study is one of the most carefully documented examinations of a self-help group. He evaluated the effectiveness of twenty-two Philadelphia TOPS chapters. He compared them with each other and with fourteen groups of obese patients treated by medical means. A composite picture of the average TOPS member is a forty-two-year-old woman (nationally, 99 percent of the TOPS members are women), weighing 188 pounds—which is 58 percent over her ideal weight, according to the standard tables. She remains in TOPS for sixteen and a half months and loses fifteen pounds during that time.

Results—expressed as a percent of members who lost twenty or more pounds—varied greatly among the twenty-two TOPS chapters, ranging from 62 percent to 12 percent. Similarly, the results reported by the fourteen medical studies also varied. Comparing the two groups, Stunkard (1972, p. 144) reports that

The results achieved by the single most effective TOPS chapter were better than those of any of the reported medical studies. The five most effective TOPS chapters ranked with the best in the medical literature. The average for all TOPS chapters was similar to the average achieved by medical treatment. Finally, the five least effective TOPS chapters and the single least effective chapter ranked with the poorest medical results.

These comparisons offer strong evidence of the effectiveness of TOPS, since the medical results with one exception are not those of the average practitioner but were obtained by physicians specializing in the treatment of obesity.

The TOPS meetings follow a standard format, patterned after Esther Manz' initial Milwaukee chapter. In many ways, they resemble AA meetings. Groups are led by a leader elected for one year. Meetings begin with a pledge or song attesting to the common goal of "controlling emotions" (Wagonfeld and Wolowitz, 1968), similar to the recitation of AA's "Twelve Steps." Then there is an announcement of each person's weight gain or loss; "the announcement is done this way so as to focus attention on immediate past performance" (Stunkard, 1972, p. 146), akin to AA's one-day-at-a-time approach. Announcements of weight loss are met with support, applause, and prizes, while weight gains are booed or jeered, or the member is otherwise made to feel disapproval. One of the studies emphasizes that in addition to the group identification and support there is a "theme of aggression which is played out among members" (Wagonfeld and Wolowitz, 1968, p. 251). As with Recovery groups, there is both competition with and cooperation among members. Although its central office plays a stronger role in relation to the individual groups than does AA's central office, TOPS' maintenance of an independent stance (it has no affiliations with other groups, it is nonprofit, and a bare 1 percent [Stunkard, 1972] to 3 percent [Wagonfeld and Wolowitz, 1968] of its members came as a result of doctor's referrals) seems to be a strong factor in its effectiveness.

Primary Care. There is no sharp line between the groups we have grouped together as providing rehabilitation (United Ostomy, International Laryngectomee, Reach to Recovery, and the heart and stroke clubs) and those included in the following section as providing primary care. For example, our discussion here of groups for hemophiliacs could as well have been included in the earlier section. Basically, the primary care groups are concerned with chronic conditions. "The acute illness relational model and the present health care system is inadequate in dealing with adaptive problems and rehabilitative processes once the acute phase of the condition has passed and in the maintenance of well care" (Tracy and Gussow, 1976, p. 385).

The National Hemophilia Foundation. The National Hemophilia Foundation's activities run across several of our categories. The Foundation engages in the fund-raising, research, and public educational activities of Gussow and Tracy's "Type II" groups, and also is directly involved with people who have problems, which characterizes the Type I group. Moreover, the activities of the hemophiliacs exemplify self-care; that is, the hemophiliacs undertake activities that previously were performed by health care professionals. New technological developments, particularly in the development of more powerful and concentrated plasma for blood replacement, make it possible for hemophiliacs to care for themselves at home (Sergis and Hilgartner, 1972).

The care of hemophiliacs goes beyond replacement therapy to mutual aid activities. Groups of patients (there are approximately 100,000 hemophiliacs, almost all male), often with their families, meet to discuss their condition and ways of coping, as well as to provide mutual support and encouragement. This is particularly important as hemophiliacs take increasing responsibility for their own care.

Women's Health. While the other self-help activities focus on a particular condition, the women's health movement encompasses the full range of concern regarding "women's bodies, bodily processes and related health care" (Marieskind, 1976, p. 64). Marieskind distinguishes between self-help groups and the provision of curative care. The former, she describes as "a group of approximately six to ten women become a self-help clinic (or *group,* as it is less confusing to call them) meeting together for about ten weeks to exchange health information and experiences, to learn breast and vaginal self-examinations, and to learn about common gynecological conditions" (Marieskind, 1976, p. 64). In the fullest sense of the word, this is health education and prevention. "Health care services are provided by women's clinics, which in cases grow out of self-help groups" (Marieskind, 1976, p. 65); at the same time, the self-help group may continue as part of the clinic's activities. Since the establishment of the first Feminist Women's Health Center in Los Angeles by Carol Downer and Lorraine Rothman in 1971 (*West Coast Sisters,* 1971, p. 3), at least fifty women-run clinics have been founded in the United States (Hornstein, Downer, and Farber, 1976).

The roles of professional providers is sharply limited; the bulk of a patient's encounter, from the initial intake to the final counseling, is with women like herself—lay women who have learned their skills in self-help courses. "But the point is not merely to replace the doctor with more socially compatible, sympathetic providers. Within feminist health clinics, an attempt is being made to completely redefine the patient and provider roles. . . . The woman is not the object of care but an active participant; not the recipient of a commodity but a coproducer of health care" (Marieskind and Ehrenreich, 1975, pp. 39–40). These ideas have precursors in the "popular health movement" of the 1830s and 1840s, which brought together feminists and working-class radicals. "They wanted nothing less than a total redefinition of health care and health itself. . . . 'Every man his own doctor,' proclaimed the more radical wing of the movement, and they meant every woman, too" (Marieskind and Ehrenreich, 1975, p. 34).

Although there have been no comparative studies of the effect of such feminist health care, Marieskind *has* tested women's knowledge of basic anatomy and simple gynecological procedures. She compared patients who used a physician-staffed clinic, those who used one staffed by a physician-trained paramedic, and those who used a feminist self-help facility. On all four sets of questions (anatomy identification, definition of gynecological procedures, knowledge of appropriate frequency of performing procedures, and contraceptive contraindications), the women at the self-help facilities scored highest, while those served at a physician-staffed facility scored lowest. Knowledge, or the lack thereof (and overall, the women at all three of the types of facilities scored only 33 percent correct on questions of contraceptive contraindications), of course, is not automatically translated into health care. However, this lack of knowledge is especially dangerous in light of "the increasing evidence of risks attached to pill and IUD usage" (Marieskind, 1976, p. 65), and also raises serious questions about women's ability to give "informed consent" for the utilization of a contraceptive method (Fleckenstein, 1976).

A unique self-help group has developed as a consequence of what can now best be described as "misinformed consent." From the 1940s to the early 1970s, from a half to two million women were given a synthetic estrogen, diethystilbestrol (DES), then believed to help them maintain tenuous pregnancies. In 1971, a series of cases of vaginal cancer were discovered in daughters of women who had taken DES; as early as 1951, evidence had been developed as to DES' ineffectiveness in pregnancy maintenance. DES-Watch was organized by Frances Rowan of Hicksville (New York), and similar groups are now operating in Boston, Philadelphia, Los Angeles, San Francisco, Mount Pleasant (Michigan), and Springfield (Illinois). The groups publish materials alerting women and doctors about DES, conduct training of doctors in the use of the colposcope (an instrument that gives a magnified view of the vagina), and lobby for funding of the semiannual examinations necessary for the daughters of women who took DES. As a self-help group, the women provide mutual support in their concern about the risks facing their daughters, as well as for their own anger as a result of having been given a drug whose effect has proved so damaging (Brozan, 1976, p. 28).

Women's health groups are the self-help groups that best

combine the focus on the individual participant and the effort to produce systematic changes.* Community control groups in health seek to gain governance authority, expecting thereby to affect practice, but do not deal with it directly. Traditional self-help groups such as AA do their own thing, largely ignoring the public policy issues. The health self-help groups, such as United Ostomy and International Laryngectomee, basically are adjuncts to the medical practitioners. On the other hand, the women's health movement has both changed actual practice as well as challenged the overall structure of health care, at least as it affects women—challenging the very existence of the specialty of ob/gyn (obstetrics/gynecology) in the belief that it perpetuates an oppressive emphasis on the reproductive function in women's identity (Marieskind and Ehrenreich, 1975); urging that males be barred from the practice of health as relates to specifically women's issues (Seaman, 1975); proposing the establishment of a women's health school (Howell, 1975b); and challenging all of the proposed national health and insurance proposals as inimical to women's health (Lewis, 1976). The women's health efforts are thus a part of the broader women's movement, with "women who have participated in self-help groups reporting feelings of strength, a sense of self-worth, self-confidence, and an ability to be assertive. . . . And it is this sense of control over one aspect of [their lives], beginning from the self-help clinic experiences, which for so many women has led to their taking control where it is feasible over other aspects of their life" (Marieskind, 1976, pp. 65–66).

Prevention and Case Finding. We have noted that much of the activity of the women's health groups involves both secondary prevention and case finding (seeking out those with a problem). These aspects develop when women learn more about their bodies, both as knowledge useful for its own sake and its self-improving consequences, as well as for its value in understanding the conditions of a woman's health separated from the misogynist biases of gynecology. (Note, for example, the approving attitude of J. Marion Sims, the nineteenth century "father" of gynecology, toward an-

---

* A quite different sort of self-help group among women is the La Leche League, which is focused on a particular segment of the life cycle, as discussed in Chapter Two.

esthetizing women suffering from vaginismus so as to make possible a successful sexual experience for the man!) The activities of a group such as DES-Watch involve both prevention and case finding.

While much of the new work in health education is directed by professionals, the use of groups and their ability to sustain and support members is being recognized in some of the more innovative programs (Somers, 1973, 1976). And the newly enacted National Health Education and Disease Prevention Act offers the opportunity for mutual aid activities (Lynch, 1975) through its authorization of innovative programs.

Hypertension is a disorder that offers an as yet little-tapped field for self-help activities, both in terms of care and of prevention. Particularly prevalent among Blacks, high blood pressure affects approximately 19,000,000 people who remain untreated and who for the most part are symptom free. If this disorder remains untreated, however, it can be very dangerous for the kidneys and heart and can endanger the life of the individual. Finding these people and having them follow a weight-reducing and exercise program along with the regular ingestion of prescribed drugs are activities that can perhaps be undertaken best by self-help groups.

Self-Care and the Activated Patient

A corollary of the formulation that in the services the consumer is producer, is that all health care is self-care; it is, ultimately, the individual who responds, reacts, and, hopefully, recovers, even in those cases where a practitioner does something (prescribes a pill, proposes a regimen, even performs a surgical operation). The professional may doctor or nurse, but it is the patient who gets well (or not). Indeed, the role of the self is central throughout the human services, in self-education, self-caring, indeed, self-preserving. The role of the individual in his or her own well-being is so basic that we often ignore it.

More narrowly, some have defined self-care as "consumer performance of activities traditionally performed by providers" (Green, Werlin, and Schauffler, 1976, p.1). One report notes a British study finding "that some attempts at self-care and advice from others had been carried out by more than 95 percent of the patients" before coming to see the doctor and that only "20 percent of all symptom experiences result in medical contact" (Levin, 1976b, p. 70). Summarizing several studies, Levin, Katz, and Holst (1976, p. 13) "suggest that perhaps 75 percent or more of health care is undertaken without professional intervention." In a sense, self-care activities overlap those that we include in the activities of self-help and mutual aid groups. They share in common such activities as health education and training in coping skills and in the three steps Strauss describes as necessary to enable sufferers of chronic illnesses to cope with their condition—ability to read signs that portend a crisis, the ability to respond to the crisis of the moment, and the ability to establish and maintain a regimen. Levin (1976a, p. 206) defines self-care as "a process whereby a layperson functions on his/her own behalf in health promotion and prevention and in disease detection and treatment at the level of the primary health resource in the health care system." And Fry (1975) identifies four roles of self-care: health maintenance; disease prevention; self-diagnosis, self-medication, and self-treatment; and patient participation in professional services.

The mutual aid concept, of course, also includes the role of the group and the "helper-therapy" dimension. Both self-care and mutual aid activities are movements away from "mediocentrism" (health care that is medically centered) and emphasize the power (and responsibility) individuals have for their own well-being. As such, they share with the women's health movement an expression of self-empowerment.

Basic to the concept of self-care is the development of understanding of health on the part of the patient, as well as the mastery of appropriate clinical skills. In the "activated patient" formulation, patients are trained to detect and manage common medical problems, to distinguish the common from the uncommon (or that for which they can care and that which requires a doctor), and to engage in health-promoting activities. Much of the current work in the area of patient activation is based on a series of patient education courses developed by Keith W. Sehnert, director of Georgetown University's Center for Health Education. These courses have been the basis of programs in Wyoming, Idaho, Utah, Maine, Virginia, North Carolina, Minnesota, and New York (Yates, 1976,

p. 8)'; a newsletter, *"The Activated Patient,"* published by the Center; and a book by Sehnert (1975).*

The Georgetown program includes presentations in the following areas: prevention of arteriosclerosis, motor vehicle accident, cirrhosis, stroke, breast cancer, uterine cancer, and rheumatic heart disease; compliance with medical regimens; hypertension, nutrition; growth and development; common childhood illnesses; contraception, family planning, and venereal disease; medications; alcoholism; mental health and family relations; yoga; automation in health care. . . . With respect to teaching patients to perform procedures on their own behalf, the course teaches self-administered blood pressure [testing], ear wax irrigation, hyposensitization shots, and emphasizes first aid. The most interesting aspect of the course is its use of checklists for self-care of common childhood diseases. The checklists include sections on general information, important points to remember in treatment, and when to call a physician. [Green, Werlin, and Schauffler, 1976, p. 9]

The program relies heavily on decision-making protocols or algorithms. "The algorithms are visual flow-charts designed to assist consumers in determining when it is appropriate to see a physician and when to apply a well-defined (in the protocol) home treatment" (Green, Werlin, and Schauffler, 1976, p. 10).

A study of fifteen programs identified the following activities as falling "under the rubric of self-care defined as the assumption by consumers of traditional provider activities" (Green, Werlin, and Schauffler, 1976, p. 11):

1. Diagnosis of common symptoms or conditions that occur frequently but need not lead to a physician visit
2. Insulin injection
3. Urine testing
4. Breast self-examination
5. Cervical self-examination
6. First aid for common injuries

* In addition to the several publications of Sehnert and his group, a considerable body of literature on self-care has developed, much of it described in Levin, Katz, and Holst (1976). More recently, there have been published the proceedings of a conference on *Self-Help and Health* (1976) and a new magazine, *Medical Self-Care.*

7. Emergency care
8. Taking blood pressure
9. Throat culture
10. Hyposensitization injections
11. Ear wax irrigation
12. Kidney dialysis
13. Self-medication for asthmatics

While the self-care programs are for the most part initiated by physicians, recent changes in nursing theory—away from the Nightingale model of helping the helpless and toward the current themes of self-care as formalized by the Nursing Development Conference Group—have encouraged and supported self-help activities, extending even to "child-initiated care," where elementary school children decide when they need to seek care and participate in decisions on managing their problems (Lewis, 1974).

But more than changes in theory lead toward the development of self-care. Milio has assembled a broad array of data that provide the bases for self-care, including evidence (Milio, 1976, p. 2) that

1. Consumers want immediate availability of health care when they need it.
2. Large portions of consumers have accurate knowledge of serious illnesses and can accurately assess the seriousness of symptoms and the severity of illness episodes.
3. Large proportions of common illnesses are self-treated.
4. People can accurately judge the appropriate circumstances under which to seek physician care.
5. Significant proportions of all population groups seek care first from non-health personnel.

Furthermore, she notes (Milio, 1976, pp. 2–3) that much of the service people seek from doctors is not related to illness; that many of the customary forms of medical treatment have serious inherent risks; the efficacy of many services is limited; and that much of present care is fragmented, as well as costly. While these factors encourage the development of self-care, the life conditions of poor people—more ill, more seriously ill, more disabled than others—are such that self-care systems must be carefully designed. "Self-care among central city populations, or among any population which has been without adequate living conditions—*if it is going to measurably contribute to the health of the people*—cannot be conceived as an individualistic or even family enterprise isolated from the community infrastructure and its need for resources" (Milio, 1976, p. 4—emphasis in original). Self-care, then, rather than emphasizing specialized techniques and technological treatment, should emphasize the most common illnesses, be located within the community, and should focus on the relationship between the individual and others in the family, neighborhood, and community (Milio, 1976, pp. 5–8). In such a context, self-care becomes a major locus for the organizing of health care.

A broad array of factors is responsible for the rising interest in self-care. The participants in the International Symposium on the Role of the Individual in Primary Health Care (Levin, Katz, and Holst, 1976, p. 20) have identified five: "(1) the 'de-mystification' of primary medical care; (2) 'consumerism' and popular demands for increased self-control—related to anti-technology, anti-authority statements; (3) changes in life-style and rising educational levels; (4) lay concern with regard to perceived abuses in medical care; and (5) the lack of availability of professional services."

And, just as there are a broad array of factors leading toward the development of self-care, so, too, its effectuation will mean the development of "evaluative strategies that go beyond the usual measurements of the benefits of health care, [that is,] absence of disease or treatment outcomes. When health care initiatives are shared by laypersons and professionals, changes can be anticipated in the health decision-making process, in the phenomenon associated with patient dependence, and in iatrogenic effects" (Levin, Katz, and Holst, 1976, p. 4).

These broader issues carry self-care efforts beyond the standard tinkerings with the health delivery system—the corrections of the imbalance with the deployment of primary medical personnel, the innovations in health care organizations, the revisions of the focus and methods of professional education. On the one hand, a critique of the very conceptualization of health care develops as a result of the shift in focus from professional provider to layperson. At the same time, there develops the critique of the nature of care as provided, the negative effect of that practice (clinical iatrogenesis), as well as the broader negative consequences (social iatrogenesis). On the other hand, there are the contributions that self-care can make toward the achievement of both a limited and an accountable health care system (Levin, Katz, and Holst, 1976, pp. 27–28); indeed, its limitation to medical matters may be a necessary step toward holding it accountable. Finally, on the debate as to whether self-care (and mutual aid) activities are supplementary to or substitutive for currently available health care resources: What must be recognized is not only that they are supplementary to those resources but also that, fundamentally, self-care and mutual aid are the bases on which all else is built—"any alternative is [both] supportive and residual" (Levin, Katz, and Holst, 1976, p. 79).

Conclusion

As we noted at the outset of this chapter, these developments of self-help and mutual aid in health are taking place in a context that both causes these developments and reflects them. This context is, first, characterized by the growth of chronic illnesses, which requires greater patient involvement, as well as by increasing concern with the cost, efficacy, and control exerted by medical practice as presently organized. The context also involves the broad consumer movement relating to control of services, as well as of their organization, accountability, and effect. In addition, the context increasingly involves the particular concerns of special groups, including women, minorities, and low-income persons, both about the nature of services as well as about their availability and distribution. More broadly, as well as particularly, there is also the current thrust toward demystification, along with those factors that we have brought together under the label *aprofessional* (see Chapters One and Four). Of course, it is the combination of these developments that gives them special power in the present and, we believe, in the future. The development of self-help is taking place among a population increasingly older, more afflicted with chronic illness, increasingly skeptical of both the efficacy and very foundation of present technologically based medical care, increasingly concerned about cost and effect, and more and more interested in doing things for oneself, as part of a broader anti-Leviathan ethos.

The developments will play themselves out in the arenas of health care itself and of public policy. Attention is now being drawn to the following set of issues: how payment for self-help activities will relate to present reimbursement practices and might be related to a national health insurance scheme; how the operation of extended programs of self-help and self-care will relate to present and future patterns of care, especially regarding health maintenance organizations (HMOs); how programs of self-help in the areas of prevention will relate to present and new health education programs (for example, see the recently enacted National Health Promotion and Disease Prevention Act, Public Law 94–317); and what the development of self-care modalities will mean for the roles and consequent training (and retraining) of professional and paraprofessional providers. The struggles over these issues will go on simultaneously in both the health and public arenas, and developments in one will affect developments in the other.

4

How Self-Help
Works

While "hard" scientific evidence regarding the effectiveness of self-help groups is sparse, a number of "soft" indicators seem to show that many self-help groups do indeed serve their clientele effectively. There are the subjective reports of the members themselves, to the effect that they have been helped by the group experience (Grosz, 1972; Wechsler, 1960a). There is also the fact that the members continue in the group, and while this does not necessarily indicate that they are benefiting, it does imply that they are obtaining some satisfaction. There is also the fact that many professional agencies refer people to self-help groups, particularly to groups such as Alcoholics Anonymous, Gamblers Anonymous, and Recovery, Inc., which deal with behaviors that have been highly resistant to the usual professional interventions. AA reports that one member in five credits a physician or hospital for directing him or her to AA.

And stigmatized people (dwarfs, for example) derive obvious benefits from the mutual support and reinforcement that a group provides (Weinberg, 1968),* aid that seems unavailable elsewhere. As Hurvitz (1974) points out, the apparent success of peer therapy groups draws added importance from the fact that their membership lies outside Schofield's well-known "YAVIS Syndrome" (1964). (The YAVIS Syndrome refers to the fact that professional psychotherapists seem to prefer clients who are Young, Attractive, Verbal, Intelligent, and Successful. Moreover, many of the behaviors "treated" by self-help groups are highly resistant to change from typical forms of professional intervention: alcoholism, compulsive gambling, drug addiction, smoking, overeating, and so on.) Peer therapy organizations thus achieve their results with precisely the segment of the population that is least likely to benefit from professional psychotherapy.

There are, in addition, a few instances in which more objective evidence is provided, such as Stunkard's (1972) study of the weight-reducing group called TOPS, using as objective indicators loss of weight and the maintenance of that loss. Reduced recidivism is reported in programs where exoffenders work with other exoffenders (Volkman and Cressey, 1963). And AA reports that 60 percent of its members maintain sobriety for a year and 40 percent for two to twenty years; several "outside" studies confirm AA's success (for example, see Stewart, 1955; Tiebout, 1944). It is important to note that few studies offer solid objective evidence for the effectiveness of most types of profesisonal intervention. In fact, the best data probably exist with regard to paraprofessional intervention (Gartner, 1971; Gartner, Jackson, and Riessman, 1977).

The power of self-help mutual aid groups derives from the fact that they combine a number of very important properties: These

---

* One study of self-help groups in two communities, one urban and one rural, with a total of sixty-seven self-help groups, reports that "over half of the urban organizations and almost three quarters of the rural state that their most important objective is to change either (or both) the public's and their membership's image of the condition from being 'deviant' to being 'different' " (Steinman and Traunstein, 1976, p. 356).

include the helper-therapy principle, the aprofessional dimension, consumer intensivity, the use of indigenous or peer support, and the implicit demand that the individual can do something for him or herself. Self-help groups show that people need not be passive, that they have power—particularly in a group that demands they do something for each other; a group that, while permitting dependence, demands autonomy and independence; a group that, while giving support, demands action and work; a group that is not leader or professional centered, but peer centered. In essence, one of the most significant characteristics of mutual aid groups is the fact that they are *empowering* and thus potentially dealienating. They enable their members to feel and use their own strengths and their own power and to have control over their own lives. This empowering dimension is extremely important for health and mental health. In addition, many self-help groups combine these features with an ideological, antisystem bias that to some extent limits their bureaucratization and limits some of the negative consequences of institutionalization.

Let us turn now to an analysis of the mechanisms or processes that characterize self-help groups.

The Helper-Therapy Principle

One of the most powerful mechanisms in mutual aid groups is what Riessman (1965) has described as the "helper-therapy" principle. In its simplest form, this principle states that those who help are helped most. Volkman and Cressey (1963, p. 134) assert: "A group in which Criminal A joins with some noncriminals to change Criminal B, is probably most effective in changing Criminal A, not B." Cressey (1965), in discussing the social psychological foundations for using criminals to help rehabilitate criminals, talks of making the criminal who is the *agent* of change the *target* of change. In a process he calls "retroflexive reformation," he says that it is his hypothesis that such success as has been experienced by Alcoholics Anonymous, Synanon, and even "official" programs like institutional group therapy and group counseling programs is attributable to the requirement that the reformee perform the role of the reformer, thus enabling him to gain experience in the role that the group has identified as desirable (Cressey, 1965, p. 56).

Thus, an alcoholic in AA who is providing help and support to another AA member may be the one who is benefiting most, by playing this helping, giving role. Furthermore, since all members of the group play this role at one time or another, they are all benefited by this helping process. In a sense, this is true of all helpers, whether they be professionals, volunteers, or whatever, but it is more sharply true for helpers who have the same problem as the helpee, as is characteristic of mutual aid groups. While all help givers may be helped themselves in a *nonspecific* way by playing the helping role (and this is not an unimportant matter), people who have a particular problem may be helped in much more specific ways by providing help to others who have the same specific problem, whether they are alcoholics, drug addicts, smokers, underachievers, heart patients, hypertensives, diabetics, or so on. Dewar (1976, p. 81) points out that "It feels good to be the helper. It increases our sense of control, of being valued, of being capable. When children play by acting out help relationships, they are more apt to seek to play the role of the helper than of the helped. It feels better. As a person organizes more of their identity around their activities and value as a helper, it gets harder to keep them from helping. It always seems more predictable that the helpers will benefit from helping, rather than the helped."

Frederickson's report (1968) on a smoking withdrawal program states that "the most meaningful reinforcement comes to those exsmokers who accept assignments as volunteer staff. . . . Smokers seem to intuit that in accepting responsibility for helping others break the habit, they will bring into play a highly effective means of reinforcing their own nonsmoking behavior" (p. 89). And a more recent study of a health education program designed to encourage children not to smoke reports that the greatest effect was on the smoking behavior of the teachers (Rabinowitz and Zimmerlin, 1976).

In one of the few experimental studies, Kelly (1973) found that the greater and more intimate the involvement of a person in the helping process, the greater the positive effect on self-concept. The study compared twenty untrained first-year students (at a small Catholic college in rural Pennsylvania) who volunteered to work as helpers in face-to-face relationships with retarded children with two other groups of first-year students—one committed to general service projects of a less personal nature in the campus community and the other not committed to any ongoing service. The study found that students who helped others on a face-to-face basis underwent greater positive change in self-concept than did those who helped in service projects who, in turn, underwent greater change than those who did not participate as helpers at all.

Weiss (1973, p. 323), in his study of Parents Without Partners, notes that "both men and women sometimes found that contribution to the organization through service in administrative or planning roles supported their own sense of worth. Leaders referred to this phenomenon by saying 'The more you put into PWP, the more you get out of it.' " Because PWP recognized that "helping" was therapeutic, it maintained many divisions and programs responsible for their own activities: "This administrative fragmentation made it possible for an administrative position to be offered to almost any member who wanted one, if not as a director of a division, then as a program coordinator or other functionary within one" (Weiss, 1973, pp. 323–324). The same principle, of course, is operative in AA, where leadership is widely diffused; many individuals have the opportunity of playing various leadership roles.

There are numerous mechanisms postulated to explain the potential power of the helper-therapy idea. Skovholt (1974, p. 62) seeking to describe and explain the helper-therapy principle, summarizes the benefits received from helping: "(1) the effective helper often feels an increased level of interpersonal competence as a result of making an impact on another's life; (2) the effective helper often feels a sense of equality in giving and taking between himself or herself and others; (3) the effective helper is often the recipient of valuable personalized learning acquired while working with a helpee; and (4) the effective helper often receives social approval from the people he or she helps." Skovholt hypothesizes that all four factors, rather than any one, make the helper-therapy principle potent.

Skovholt further sees the helper-therapy principle as rooted in social exchange theory and the norm of reciprocity. The norm of reciprocity is a universal norm, according to Gouldner (1960); essentially, it states that people should help but not hurt those who have helped them. As a norm, reciprocity relies on an economic exchange model, in that one does not want to go into debt to another person. Skovholt suggests that in working with drug and alcoholic addicts, who typically violate the reciprocity norm by taking more than they give, the helper-therapy principle may have special significance. The strict structure of programs such as AA and Synanon, with received chores and helping of others, may have the result that "for the first time in a long time these members feel a sense of reciprocity and, therefore, satisfaction with themselves (Skovholt, 1974, p. 63).

Probably the mechanisms also vary depending on the setting and task of the helper. Helpers functioning in a therapeutic context, whether as professional therapeutic agents or as nonprofessional "peer therapists," may benefit from the importance and status associated with this role. Because relationships in a self-help setting between helper and helped usually are between persons of little status discrepancy and are such that money is not exchanged, Skovholt suggests that the exchange theory of Foa and Foa (1971) may apply. This theory points out that a social exchange does not necessarily mean a loss to one of the two parties (Foa and Foa, 1971). "The helper and helpee can . . . give to each other without either person losing. In all likelihood, the resources given to the helper (by the helpee) will be affection and esteem" (Skovholt, 1974, p. 61).

Self-Persuasion. Another dimension of the helper principle is reflected in the persuasion process itself. Helpers in the process of persuading helpees have to persuade or reinforce themselves, not in some general way, but about the various specific problems that they share in common. A study by King and Janis (1956) is relevant in this context. They found that subjects who had to improvise a speech supporting a specific point of view tended to change their opinions in the direction of this view more than did subjects who merely read the speech for an equivalent amount of time. The King-Janis study suggests that becoming committed to a position through advocating it ("self-persuasion through persuading others") may be an important dimension associated with the helper role.

Pearl (1964, p. 4) notes that many helpers (such as the homework helpers) are "given a stake or concern in a system," and this contributes to their becoming "committed to the task in a way that brings about especially meaningful development of their own abilities."

The Helping Role. There are at least three additional mechanisms to account for the fact that the person playing the helping role achieves special benefits: (1) the helper is less dependent; (2) in struggling with the problem of another person who has a like problem, the helper has a chance to observe his or her problem at a distance; and (3) the helper obtains a feeling of social usefulness by playing the helping role. The entire helper therapy concept is derived from role theory, whereby a person playing a role tends to carry out the expectations and requirements of that role. In effect, as a helper the individual displays mastery over the afflicting condition—plays the role of a nonaddict, for example— and thereby acquires the appropriate skills, attitudes, behaviors, and mental set. Having modeled this for others, the individual may see him- or herself as behaving in a new way and may, in effect, take on the new role as his or her own.

Helpers also receive support from the implicit thesis "I must be well if I can help others." There is also an explicit reward in helping others, in having an impact on another person's life, in reducing another's suffering. Moreover, the helper role may function as a major *distracting* source of involvement, thus diverting helpers from their own problems and a general overconcern with self. There is also no question that individual differences are important, so that some people receive much greater satisfaction than do others from giving, helping, leading, persuading, and nurturing.

The Best Way to Learn Is to Teach

The helper-therapy principle can perhaps be most easily recognized in examining the well-known tutoring studies, of children teaching other children. Considerable evidence indicates that it is the child who is doing the teaching or tutoring who is most clearly benefited (Allen, 1976; Gartner, Kohler, and Riessman, 1971; Newmark, 1976).

While programs of children learning from their peers are documented as far back as ancient Rome, it is more recently that the emphasis has been placed on the benefits that may accrue to the tutor. In the early 1960s, Peggy and Ronald Lippitt (and associates) studied the effects of using older elementary and junior high school students with younger elementary grade children. The Lippitts focused on the process of socialization among the older children and assistance to the younger children (Lippitt, Eiseman, and Lippitt, 1969).

Working at Mobilization for Youth (MFY—a New York City antipoverty program that employed an extensive tutoring system whereby high school youngsters were prepared to tutor disadvantaged elementary school children), Frank Riessman (1965) observed that, although the tutees enjoyed the tutoring sessions, no great improvement occurred in their learning. On the other hand, the tutors appeared to be "turned on" by what they were doing. They were not only becoming excited about it and deriving new, heightened self-esteem from their efforts, but they also seemed much more interested in the whole learning process. They were evidently acquiring new "sets," skills and attitudes that were being transferred to many other learning experiences in which they were involved. Thus, a tutor teaching arithmetic to an elementary school youngster showed self-improvement not only in mathematics, but also in other subjects. Moreover, in many cases the tutors appeared to acquire a new self-conscious, analytic orientation in dealing with all kinds of problems, not just academic work.

These impressionistic observations led MFY's research staff, in particular Robert Cloward and his associates, to develop carefully controlled studies to assess what was occurring. They found striking gains in the achievement scores of the tutors, gains that far exceeded those of the tutees. For example, over a five-month period in which older children tutored younger children having reading difficulties, those tutored gained 6.0 months (in standardized reading level), while the tutors gained an extraordinary 3.4 years (Cloward, 1967). Unfortunately, most of the cognitive measures employed, not only at MFY but elsewhere, have thus far been largely restricted to achievement tests. A great need exists to develop new, expanded indices related to learning how to learn, creativity, analytic thinking, curiosity, and the like.

Since these beginnings in the early 1960s, there has been an enormously rapid spread of various types of tutorial programs. In 1968 Herbert Thelen listed some two dozen programs, each conducted by a school as part of its regular day. The National Commission on Resources for Youth, under the guidance of Mary Conway Kohler, has developed "Youth-Tutoring-Youth" programs that began with demonstration projects in Newark and Philadelphia in 1967 and that are now in operation in over 600 school systems. And the Office of Education's Career Opportunities Program, which operated in some 130 communities in all fifty states, incorporated a Youth-Tutoring-Youth component designed by the Commission (Carter, 1976).

In Pacoima, California, an entire school was involved in the development of a tutorial community project (Newmark, 1976). In Portland, Oregon, most of the children in the high schools are engaged in an assisting program. And under a grant from the Teacher Corps, the New Careers Training Laboratory, City University of New York, and Community School District 5 are fashioning a schoolwide learning-by-teaching program at Public School 133 in Central Harlem. Elsewhere, tutoring programs focus on children with special handicaps, sometimes using "problem children" and "disabled" children as tutors. In some cities, programs with classes composed of children of several ages (interage classes) use tutoring as a part of the regular class activity.

Apart from the affective, ego-enhancing benefits obtained by the child playing the tutoring role, there are clearly cognitive benefits as the child learns to learn and, in presenting the material to the younger tutee, has to learn the material better him- or herself, has to review it, prepare it, reformulate it, organize it, individualize it, and provide examples. As the tutor reshapes or reformulates the material so as to enable the tutee to learn it, the tutor comes to see it in new ways; he or she may need to seek out the basic character of the subject, its structure, in order to teach it better and may thereby understand it better. A quote from Jerome Bruner is most interesting in this regard: "I went through it (quantum theory) once and looked up only to find the class full of blank faces—they had obviously not understood. I went through it a second time and they still did not understand it. And so I went through a third time, and that time I understood it" (cited in Gartner, Kohler, and Riessman, 1971, p. 81). In addition, of course, there are the affective benefits derived from playing the role of helper: the ego improvement, the building of greater self-respect, the fact that one is doing something important and useful and developing a competence, and the need to model for someone else, as well as seeing the problem in new ways, because of not being a passive recipient, but an active helper.

The implication of all this—and this maxim is of course implicitly and perhaps unconsciously followed by practically all mutual aid groups—is that everyone who needs help should have the opportunity of playing the helper role, whether that person be a child in school who is underachieving, an alcoholic, or a drug addict. *The human service strategy ought to be to devise ways of creating more helpers.* Or to be more exact, the strategy ought to find ways to transform recipients of help into new dispensers of help, thus reversing their roles, and to structure the situation so that recipients of help will be placed in roles requiring the giving of assistance. The helper-therapy principle operates, of course, in all kinds of peer help situations, in peer counseling in schools, children teaching children, or mutual help groups. Therefore, all situations involving human service should be restructured to allow the principle to work more fully.

Since the problems faced by youth are more a part of what Erikson (1959) has identified as the development crisis common to adolescence, than are the chronic conditions of alcoholics, laryngectomees, and the like, mutual aid groups are a way both to cope with the problems of youth and to learn how to build new ways of living, growing, working, and relating. At the same time, mutual aid among youth may partake of other characteristics of adolescence—overattending to the crisis of the moment, introverting, and rejecting all authority or prior experience. Where the problems of the individual are serious, the group process may become a forum for projecting, avoiding, and self-deceiving, especially since, as with any voluntary group, those involved in self-help groups are a self-selected body, as are the professionals who choose to work with them. The mutual aid peer groups are a way for adolescents to find themselves and others, as well as a way to learn new behaviors.

They may tend to reject authority and past experience as irrelevant, authoritarian, and "not of us." There may be little sense of a dialectic between present subjective experience and external knowledge. (To some extent, all this is true of all self-help groups, as a type.)

Consumer as Producer

An important aspect of self-help groups is the special involvement of consumers. In all the services, as we pointed out in Chapter One, the consumer plays a unique role, contributing to the productivity of the service and of the practitioner. The consumer thus is potentially a producer and, to the extent that he or she is used more fully as a producer, this involvement contributes to the effectiveness of the service.

Consumer involvement not only affects quantity, but also has an important and fundamental effect on the quality of all human services, whether the service be education, health care, or mental health. This is because so much of *the essence of the human services depends on the involvement and motivation of the consumer*. Children's learning depends, in the last analysis, on their becoming involved, learning how to learn, getting turned on, becoming won to learning; an individual's health depends on what he or she does about maintaining it, preventing illness, and building positive health. As Tyler (1976, pp. 444) points out, "In this respect, health care, education, and treatment cannot be delivered by someone else." And in overcoming most of the behavior-related disorders of our time, such as smoking, alcoholism, and drug addiction, it is obvious that the consumer's self-involvement is decisive. There are countless other illustrations of this in sex therapy, parenting, psychotherapy, family planning, and recreation. In all these cases, the individual consumer's involvement powerfully affects the character and *quality* of the service. Clearly, in the self-help approach, the consumers are primary not only in helping themselves, but also in helping and serving others like themselves. The self-help approach represents the essence of consumer involvement in that the role of the professional service provider is, at most, minimal.

Consumer-intensive involvement, of course, occurs not only in self-help groups, but also in a great variety of other areas where the consumer input is critical. In all of the so-called coping books—on assertiveness training, sex therapy, transcendental meditation, dieting, and relaxation techniques—the consumer is obviously the decisive force in helping him- or herself, and the professional input is restricted to the input coming from the book. Similarly, in the various parent training courses, although they are run by professionals for a fee and thus do not fit our mutual aid definition, there is significant consumer involvement. "Parents find talking about their problems to a sympathetic audience cathartic, and hearing about problems they don't have reassuring." And there is "the exhilarating feeling that one is no longer alone—that all parents are in the same boat, whether they can row it or not" (Brown, 1976, p. 48).

The Aprofessional Dimension

The important thing about the self-help groups, however, is that they combine consumer involvement with the helper-therapy principle and the aprofessional dimension. The following chart, developed by Nathan Hurvitz (1974, pp. 28–29), presents an interesting contrast between orthodox (professional) psychotherapy and self-help (largely aprofessional) group therapy. (For a fuller expression of these contrasts, see Appendix B.)

Professional Psychotherapy	*Self-Help Group Therapy*
1. Professional, authoritative therapy.	1. Nonprofessional leaders; group parity.
2. Fee.	2. Free.
3. Appointments and records.	3. None.
4. Therapy-oriented milieu (psychiatrist's office, clinic, and so on).	4. Nontherapy-oriented milieu (church rooms, community centers, and so on).
5. No family confrontation.	5. Family encouraged.
6. Psychiatrist is presumed normal; does not identify with patient.	6. Peers are similarly afflicted; identify with each other.

7. Therapist is not a role model; does not set personal examples.

7. Peers are role models; must set examples for each other.

8. Therapist is noncritical, nonjudgmental, neutral, listens.

8. Peers are active, judgmental, supportive, critical, talk.

9. Patients unilaterally divulge to therapist; disclosures are secret.

9. Peers divulge to each other; disclosures are shared.

10. Patients expect only to receive support.

10. Patients must also give support.

11. Concerned about symptom substitution if underlying causes are not removed.

11. Urges appropriate behavior; not concerned about symptom substitution.

12. Accepts disruptive behavior and sick role; absolves patient; blames cause.

12. Rejects disruptive behavior and sick role; holds member responsible.

13. Therapist does not aim to reach patient at "gut level."

13. Peers aim to reach each other at "gut level."

14. Emphasis on etiology, insight.

14. Emphasis on faith, willpower, self-control.

15. Patient's improvement is randomly achieved.

15. Patient's behavior is planfully achieved.

16. Therapist–patient relationship has little direct community impact.

16. Peers' intersocial involvement has considerable community impact.

17. Everyday problems subordinated to long-range cure.

17. Primary emphasis on day-to-day victories: another day without liquor or drugs, another day without panic, and so on.

18. Extracurricular contact and socialization with psychiatrist discouraged.

18. Continuing support and socialization available.

19. Lower cumulative dropout percentage.

19. Higher dropout percentage.

20. Patient cannot achieve parity with psychiatrist.

20. Members may themselves become active therapists.

It becomes clear from examining these characteristics that the mutual aid groups use much more subjective, peer, informal, gut-level approaches; disclosures are shared and the participants are judgmental with each other. In essence, the self-help approach reflects a series of dimensions that might be termed *aprofessional*. The professional is much more concerned with a systematic, knowledge-based approach; with the need for distance and perspective; with empathy perhaps, but not identification; with objectivity rather than subjectivity; with practice based on scientific analysis, rather than experience or intuition; and with praxis rather than practice—that is, theoretically directed reflective practice, rather than simply practice alone. By contrast, in self-help groups among addicted populations, for example, the addict is asked to play a new role (and is supported in doing so), without requiring that he or she understand it. This focus on doing, this emphasis on behavior, characterizes all of the self-help groups.

In the following chart, we present a schematic, ideal-type contrast between the professional and the aprofessional modes of human service.

Professional	*Aprofessional*
1. Emphasis on knowledge and insight, underlying principles, theory, and structure.	1. Emphasis on feeling and affect (concrete, practical).
2. Systematic.	2. Experience, common sense intuition, and folk knowledge are central.
3. "Objective"—use of distance and perspective, self-awareness; control of "transference."	3. Subjective—closeness and self-involvement.
4. Empathy; controlled warmth.	4. Identification.
5. Standardized performance.	5. Extemporaneous, spontaneous (expressions of own personality).
6. "Outsider" orientation.	6. "Insider" orientation; indigenous.

7. Praxis.   7. Practice.
8. Careful, limited use of time;   8. Slow; time no issue; informal,
   systematic evaluation; curing.   direct accountability; caring.

The aprofessional dimension is not only a powerful counter-balance to the intrinsic limitations of professional intervention, but it also serves to reduce some of the difficulties in professional approaches that are not intrinsic, but rather that are related to the way the professional functions in our society. We are referring to professional elitism—the tendency to mystify, to maintain a monopoly and high cost for professional service, to be removed, particularly from low-income and rural populations, to not be sufficiently accountable and relevant to the consumer, and to frequently apply outmoded practices because these are the ones in which professionals have been trained.

Any aprofessional approach is likely to be much more consumer centered, immediately relevant, demystified, credible, not held in an imperialistic manner, nonelitist, more directly accountable to the consumer, at least in terms of direct satisfaction, and, of course, far less expensive. Many of the characteristics of the professional, of course, may not be endemic to the professional role, but rather to that role in various social structures in certain historical periods. However, there is some tendency for various of these extrinsic characteristics of the professional—the elitism, mystification, and so on—to be universal, as is indicated by the powerful effort of the Chinese cultural revolution to reduce these behaviors in a society that had been socialist for some period of time.

There is a derivative dimension of this issue, most dramatically seen in the mental health field, that is of some interest. Fuller Torrey, in his illuminating description of the universal components of psychotherapy (1972), notes that a number of characteristics, such as a shared world view, patient expectations, and personal qualities of the therapist, are decisive in the therapeutic process. Whatever intellectual rationale is utilized, these dimensions, while varying in form from culture to culture, appear to be the significant dimensions in the psychotherapeutic intervention. It is clear that a consumer-based approach, such as the self-help modality, provides a much wider range of connections to the client's world view, expectations, or systems of belief than does any of the more abstract professional models. The professional model has a whole series of assumptions and an underlying world view that do not easily connect to the large numbers of consumers, who prefer for their mental health intervention the world views of religion or astrology or the new therapies, such as encounter, EST, assertiveness training, the coping books, and the self-help movement. While this point is most clearly perceived in relation to mental health intervention, it is also true to varying degrees in the other human services, such as health and education. Thus some people require the scientific superstructure, language, vocabulary, and assumptions of a formal medical system and the accompanying doctor, but others are much more drawn to various non-Western approaches, based on a different set of assumptions and value frames. The point we are making here is that the self-help approach and the aprofessional dimension allows for a much wider range of intervention formats, tying in with different consumers' systems of thought. The self-help aprofessional approach often draws on an activist orientation based more on the assumptions of the value of will and faith than on knowledge and understanding. Not only are these dimensions probably useful in any human service intervention, but they also fit in more fully with the orientations of many groups in the population who are less accepting of the professional stress on understanding as the main avenue to change and improvement.

Truax and Carkhuff (1973) point out that much of the professionals' training and socialization move them away from the dimensions of identification, deep concern, full involvement, and caring, which often derive from nearness to the client, from feeling like the client in a highly direct, indigenous fashion. Actually, indigenousness, a characteristic emphasized a great deal in the 1960s with the development of the paraprofessional movement, is a very important component of the aprofessional dimension. The word *indigenous* means "coming from," "a part of," "close to," "near"— the community or clients to be served. And while this nearness may result, at times, in overidentification and an impairment of perspective, it also contains a valuable component in human service practice.

The Role of the Group Process

In addition to the dimensions already mentioned, of course, one of the most obvious factors related to the effectiveness of self-help groups stems from the group process itself. Clinard (1963, p. 647) states that "In each case, the group helps to integrate the individual, to change his conception of himself, to make him feel again the solidarity of the group behind the individual, and to combat social stigma. These group processes, it is felt, replace 'I' feelings with 'we' feelings, give the individual the feeling of being in a group, and redefine certain norms of behavior."

The group provides support, reinforcement, sanctions, and norms; extends the power of the individual; provides peer help; sets limits; enables its members to share; provides feedback; and occupies time. While this last might normally be thought of as a negative, for a person seeking to overcome addictive behavior that had come to control *and* occupy one's entire life, involvement in the group helps to fill time and to replace the activities involved in the addiction. It is not uncommon, for example, for alcoholics to attend AA meetings many nights a week, both to give and get help.

Katz (1970b) provides a useful overview of some of the processes of self-help that are related to the group:

1. Peer or primary group reference identification.
2. Facilitation of communication because members are peers.
3. Enhanced opportunities for socialization.
4. Breaking down of individual psychological defenses through group action, open discussion, and confrontation.
5. Provision of an acceptable status system within which the member can achieve his place. Status is defined according to group goals and needs, and the individual's status within the social system of the group can be relatively clearly defined.
6. Simulation of or proximity to conditions of the outside world in the groups, as compared with the institutional setting or professional client–practitioner relationship.

These factors are particularly significant for people who have been excluded, for whatever reason, from society's mainstream. In the self-help setting, they can experience normal social contacts, as well as communication that is unhampered by irrelevant barriers. Most important, they can experience the opportunity for leadership. Although a self-help group or network may include professional or volunteer participation, or may even be the result of a human service worker's initial prodding, its potential for success is based on the active participation and commitment of its members. Those members must know that there is "room at the top."

Lewis and Lewis (1976) characterize self-help groups as comparable to Almond's "healing community" (Almond, 1974). The healing community is seen as being therapeutic, both in terms of the interpersonal relationships among individual members and in terms of the social structure of the group as a whole. The therapeutic, or curative, aspects of individual relationships are defined as "healing charisma," meaning that there is a specialness in the quality of person-to-person interaction, a social energy that helps members to experience themselves as people who can "actually become what they would like to become." The social structure of the group as a whole is characterized by "communitas." This means that individuals are not given status according to particular roles or titles but, ideally, that all of the individuals and all of their relationships are "charismatic" and joined by a basic "relatedness." "The ideal of the healing community is for each individual and every interpersonal relationship to be charismatic. Communitas inspires feelings by emphasizing basic equality and integral relatedness among members; charisma strengthens the communitas by providing a form for relatedness that is special and not dependent on rigidly defined social structures" (Almond, 1974, p. xxx). When new members enter the healing community, they are encouraged to believe that the group and all its members are special and that they can share in this quality. Full membership is valued and is seen as a result of behavior that is modeled according to the particular norms of the group. The same kind of behavior is expected from every member of the group, and it is through that behavior that an initiate becomes a full-fledged group member, a care giver instead of solely a care receiver. In a group such as Synanon, members are expected to move in fully—not only physically but also in soul, to cut ties to the outside, to focus all of their attention and activities within the community.

While we have emphasized the alikeness of the members of the group, of course, there is a key difference among members, between oldtimers and newcomers. In discussing the helper-therapy concept, we have noted that the oldtimers benefit in the process of helping others. But there is benefit, too, for the newcomers. Festinger (1954) has argued that individuals are most influenced by persons whom they perceive as like themselves. Antze (1976, p. 326) supports this view: "The strongest influencers are those whom the subject sees as like himself." For example, in the statement of the oldtimer at an AA meeting that he is an alcoholic, but obviously under control, the new member sees what he himself can become. And, of course, the conviction as to the rightness of the groups' way is most ingrained in that successful oldtimer, and the newcomer is affected by the members with the strongest convictions.

Ideology

A further aspect of many of the self-help groups is their ideological character. Ideology goes beyond the activity of the individual to involvement in something beyond oneself, to a broader commitment, and to social change. This is perhaps most obvious in women's and men's consciousness-raising groups and in parent groups that have worked for better conditions for their handicapped children. But it is also operative in the various deviant and stigmatized groups, such as gays, former offenders, stutterers, midgets, and other social outcasts, where the ideology of the group involves criticism of society and the demand for social change. This criticism is frequently directed at professionals and social agencies, as well as at the larger society. The ideological perspective of the self-help group gives it force and conviction in dealing with these agencies and in feeling much more positively about itself and its condition.

Antze (1976), using the term *ideology* in a slightly different fashion, believes that the ideological aspect is critical to the effectiveness of the self-help groups. He calls this the "persuasive function" of the groups. "Each claims a certain wisdom concerning the problem it treats. Each has a specialized system of *teachings* that members venerate as the secret of recovery. These are often codified in a book recited in capsule form at the start of each meeting. I have chosen to label such teachings 'ideologies.' In the present context . . . this term includes not only the groups explicit beliefs, but also its rituals, rules of behavior, slogans, and even favorite terms of phrase" (Antze, 1976, p. 324). He argues that the persuasive function of the ideology operates as a "cognitive antidote" to basic features of a condition shared by everyone who joins the group.

Antze analyzes the ways in which the ideology plus certain structural characteristics of self-help groups play a major role in blocking relapse and achieving conversion without ever dealing with "underlying causes." He notes that

> The sharing of experience so widely practiced in these groups plays a central role in this process. As even brief observation at meetings will show, the stories that members tell each other are scarcely flat, "objective" reports. Every narrative presents experience from a point of view, and it is often discussed with great care. Thus, either overtly or tacitly, the story becomes an object lesson, an illustration of certain ideas. In this sense, the sharing of experience runs well beyond confession or catharsis to operate as a subtle form of indoctrination. . . . evidence on the influencing process suggests that the persuasive effect here is likely to be strongest for the person telling the story, since he is actively recasting his experience in the light of the group's ideas.
>
> To some extent, peer therapy groups draw their persuasiveness from the kinds of problems they treat. A great many of these groups address conditions of an extreme and terrifying kind so that prospective members often arrive in states approaching despair. With their former lives in complete disarray, these sufferers are only too ready to embrace a new system of ideas that promises relief or comfort. [Antze, 1976, p. 326]

To this point, we have presented this discussion of the mechanisms involved in mutual help as if they were the same for all groups—they are not, of course. Among some groups one particular feature may be more important than others. In comparing AA, Recovery, Inc., and Synanon, Antze (1976, p. 344) notes that "each of the organizations . . . achieves its effects by counteracting certain key attitudes that typify its client group. Thus, AA counters the assertiveness of alcoholics by teaching surrender; Recovery, Inc., blocks the habitual surrender of ex-mental patients by promoting willpower; and Synanon reverses the addict's social and emotional detachment through a process that expresses feelings and strengthens social engagement."

Conclusion

The power of mutual help groups is related to the fact that they combine a number of very important properties: the aprofessional dimension, consumer intensivity, the helper-therapy principle, persuasion, ideology, the role of the group, and the process of commitment.

The range of support that self-help groups provide is broad, including support for the child-abusing mother who needs someone to share a "bad" afternoon, the alcoholic who needs support not to take the first drink, the widow who needs someone to help maintain contact with the outside world, and the laryngectomee who needs extensive assurance that life can regain some semblance of normalcy. Yet Durman (1976, p. 435) points out that "The common theme in these and other examples which could be cited is the need for human interaction, available quickly in crisis, at all hours, for potentially long periods of time, and in which the focus is not basic change in outlook or personality, but in sustaining the ability to cope with a difficult situation."

Many of the other self-help approaches—for example, the coping books—while not partaking of the group dimension, use important self-help mechanisms, such as aprofessionality and consumer intensivity. They are, thus, important in the human services repertoire. The special importance of self-help mutual aid groups is that they combine these features with the group process and, frequently, with an antisystem bias.

5

Potentials and Limitations of Self-Help

Although the self-help movement has enormous potential, there are inherent in it a number of potential dangers that are particularly exacerbated in the current climate of scarcity and economizing. One danger is that self-help approaches may be offered as substitutes for the expansion of paid services. Some argue not only that the traditional services are expensive and unproductive, but also that their professional character is detrimental. The aprofessional, self-help approach is therefore proposed as an alternative, rather than a complement, to needed human services. To some extent, this substitution has already taken place, through the use of volunteers.

The problem is worsened by the fact that employed workers

may be thrown against the self-help participants, just as employed workers are sometimes pitted against the volunteers, creating divisiveness and competitiveness where cooperation and collegiality are essential. Historic examples of this difficulty are plentiful. For example, in the nineteenth-century Lancaster movement in England, children tutoring other children was used as a cost-saving device directed toward replacing teachers with child tutors. The children-teaching-children approach in the present period requires at least as many paraprofessionals, teachers, and supervisors as are now involved in education in order to organize it properly and relate it to the mainstream school learning. If it is used as a substitute for educational personnel, its great potential will surely be lost, and the antagonism created would be a disaster.

A derivative danger is the possiblity of victim blaming* as a diversion from system and professional responsibility. This danger is inherent in all consumer- or client-oriented forms of intervention, from the bootstrap approaches that are offered to the poor and minority groups, all the way to approaches proposing that inflation be halted by consumers withholding their dollars. These approaches divert energy away from the structural and system-oriented transformations that are necessary to deal with inflation or to improve health, housing, education, and mental health. Any client-centered approach tends to deemphasize larger societal issues. Although self-help approaches in the health field, for example, are important for the improvement of the health of the nation, so are the development of occupational safety, housing, job security, environmental pollution, and national health insurance. It behooves the self-help movement to be very aware of this tendency and to counteract it actively, as do the groups that are concerned with social action, such as the women's groups, the exoffenders, and the parents of retarded children. These groups are concerned with legislative changes as well as with their immediate lot.

Ralph Nader and his supporters warn that self-help ap-

---

* Because some self-help groups portray themselves as rock bottom, for persons who have tried everything else, individuals who drop out of a group because of their own real or assumed limitations or those of the group "may devalue themselves and develop a stronger negative self-concept. This may be especially true for those who joined the group believing it was the last possible source of help" (Hurvitz, 1974, p. 95).

proaches detract from the need for system responsibility, that they encourage demands to "clean your own streets, rather than demand better service by the sanitation department," and to "get rid of crime in your neighborhood by organizing your own block patrols, rather than obtain improved police protection." Actually, this bootstrap approach has long been directed at poor and minority groups, who have been told "the way out of your condition is to pull yourself up by your own bootstraps rather than to demand better economic opportunities."

The dilemma for these groups is that in the context of a lack of service, limited economic opportunities, and the like it is perfectly natural to take matters into one's own hands, to form one's own groups and to deal with one's own problems, using one's own resources. Much of the self-help movement, of course, has arisen because of uncorrected failures in the larger system and the service agencies. AA spreads because professional agencies are not able to deal effectively with or are not sufficiently interested in the alcoholic client; exoffenders band together to help themselves because the system discriminates against and stigmatizes them. And on and on goes the list, from stutterers to dwarfs to Parents Without Partners to dying patients, all of whom have been poorly served by the overall system. There is no question that by providing their own services such groups reduce pressure on the system for the needed structural changes; on the other hand, if they did not provide these services and the system did not change immediately, the services would be sorely lacking. This is a constant dilemma.

In extreme form, an overemphasis on the self rather than on the social structure can lead to escapism, narcissism, and privatism—dangers that are enhanced in the current scarcity-oriented era, where large numbers of people retreating from the hopeful, expansionary 1960s are increasingly apt to believe that nothing can be done about the larger society. They therefore claim that "small is beautiful," and so the small group and ultimately the self become the centers of concern. Some retreat entirely from the larger agenda; others, with varying degrees of consciousness, seem to believe that the changes developing in the small units and in the self will somehow add up to or contagiously spread to major societal transformation. How this will occur is rather vague, and it is certainly difficult to point to any illustrations where it has in fact taken place. In a sense, this type of thinking reflects a continuation of the limited scope of the 1960s, in which interpersonal and cultural changes completely overshadowed the need for large-scale economic and political changes. Since the latter never occurred, the former remained limited, encapsulated, and frustrated. Some of the romantic zeal of the 1960s has been shifted to the small group, mutual aid agenda. It would seem, however, that unless the self-help movement is connected to larger social issues—as it is, for example, in the women's movement, which has increasingly been concerned with issues such as full employment and guaranteed jobs—the self-help orientation will remain no stronger than the interpersonal, cultural, and sexual revolutions of the 1960s.

The romantic anarchy and nihilism of Ivan Illich and many of the other decentralizing, deinstitutionalizing theorists needs to be counterbalanced by concern for the larger questions, such as the need for national economic planning. While there is an enormous role for decentralized local participation and small group forms, these must be integrated with changes of national scope. Small is beautiful only if it is a part of what is large and functional. If this rule is ignored, we will get the vulgarization of the Schumacher (1973) position, in which national governmental responsibility is rejected in favor of a vague, ephemeral, beautiful small unit.

It is interesting to contrast self-help and small group participation as it exists in China with the model emerging in the United States. In the Chinese situation, the small community participation emphasis is counterbalanced by a powerful monolithic state that touches it and subtly controls it at every point. Of course, this is not a model that we would like to imitate in the United States, nor could we; but the connecting of small group participation to a national agenda is necessary, minus the monolithic dimension. The achievement of this unity is difficult, and probably has not yet been achieved anywhere, but unless we move in this direction we are destined to suffer the frustrations of the small group, world orientation on the one hand, or bureaucratic statism on the other. The latter is the more obvious evil at the moment, and so people look hopefully to the small group and the individual as the answer to all of their problems, forgetting the balance and integration that is needed.

There are a variety of other difficulties in the self-help approach. Most of the traditional self-help approaches in mental health and in other human service fields have been directed largely to middle-class groups and, at times, to upper-working-class groups. This leaves the poor underserved by both the traditional agencies and the self-help groups. This is particularly surprising in light of the deep self-help traditions among the poor and particularly in light of the way these traditions have been expressed in relation to social action, welfare rights, tenants groups, neighborhood mutual aid, and the like. We need to build on these traditions and to expand the various health and mental health modalities in the self-help field to be applicable for poor people, who suffer from various problems, such as hypertension, in disproportionate numbers. It will be important, for example, to see whether the self-help approach (or philosophy) can affect the way health care is "provided" under National Health Insurance. Will it be the standard doctor-centered health care, or will it be more participatory and deprofessionalized?

Neighborhood paraprofessionals may be key agents in developing self-help approaches for low-income populations who have been hitherto underserved. But here another danger rears its ugly head, and that is that the poor may get self-help, while the rich get professional services. Both groups need both kinds of services.

Not only are there difficulties in terms of what self-help does not do, but there is also the opposite danger of it trying to do too much or trying to be all things to all people. Jencks (1976), in discussing self-help in health, notes eleven different constituencies (present or potential) for the development of self-help activities. These include the self-help groups themselves, consumers interested in participating, public health planners, physicians, nurses, critics of technocratic society, egalitarians, humanizers, fiscal planners, consumer action groups, and community control advocates. He points out that among the wide array of supporters there are major areas of conflict (present or potential). For example, the interests of fiscal planners who see self-help as a way to cut costs will conflict with the views of egalitarians and social activists; physicians

who view self-help as a way to avoid dealing with patients whom
they do not wish to see will be in conflict with consumer action
groups who fear that patients will be ignored; the efforts of social
activists to transform the self-help effort with wider reform will
turn off government, insurance payers, and some consumers; what
will be viewed as a criterion of success for one group—for example,
cutting emergency room visits among asthmatics—may be viewed
by others as a way of avoiding giving services to an "undesirable"
group (Jencks, 1976, pp. 87–89).

Professionalized Clients and the Medicalization of Life

Dewar (1976) warns that among self-helpers are large numbers of those whom he labels "professionalized clients." That is,
"rather than offering a substantially different alternative to professional services, they seek to 'service' themselves and their fellows as
they were once 'serviced' by professional helpers. Rather than
changing the content of the help, they merely alter *who* does it.
Rather than learning about and dealing with the *cause* of the
condition in question, they seize control of currently accepted professional 'cures' (Dewar, 1976, p. 79). It is not that these "professionalized clients" take on the status or authority of the professional; rather, they become socialized to thinking in a professional
mode. They define the care system as does the professional: Health
is something you "get," not "do"; a body is something you "have"
and not "are" (Dewar, 1976, p. 79).

The danger of professionalized clients is that they are more
concerned with how they feel, or with who is helping, than with
what works. They do not look to causes (environmental factors,
economic circumstances, genetic endowment, and individual and
group behavior), but to what makes them feel better (Dewar, 1976,
p. 81). They apply professional solutions as a reflex and thus are
only as effective or appropriate as the professionals they mimic. In
actuality, they expand professional hegemony and constitute a
political illusion. "Self-help and mutual aid groups, by their emphasis on specific problems, emphasize and reinforce those problems
rather than making clear that they are an integral part of total

human and community life. Human services, including those provided by self-help groups, have, by their emphasis on therapeutic intervention, turned themselves into staples in our society; people are increasingly convinced that they are unable to live their lives without professional advice or aid from others afflicted with the same problem, that they must react to life experiences as they are taught by 'experts,' whether professional or not, to react. Our language, of course, tells us something of where we are; we now speak of 'coping' to refer to what was once called 'living' " (Sidel and Sidel, 1976, p. 68).

Of course, such developments are not solely the cause of the self-help groups. Indeed, there is "a tendency among professionals to *'problemize'* the needs presented by a client, that is, to assume that the client's immediate concern—paying the rent, argument with a spouse—are symptoms of a deeper 'problem' requiring both extensive and intensive intervention. An alternative viewpoint would attempt to *'normalize'* the situation by seeing it as reflective of relatively immediate circumstances and requiring simple, direct, and nonintensive treatment" (Durman, 1976, p. 436).

The crisis of contemporary professionalism runs deeper than just how we are made to feel by our helpers. Fundamentally, it turns on the question of *what works.* If the results of professional servicing were substantial enough or even more predictable, people would be more willing to put up with feeling badly—provided it led to results worth having. But the results have been disappointing.

A number of other criticisms have been leveled at self-help mutual aid approaches: Frequently they foster dependence, sometimes life-long dependence, on the part of the participants; some of them are authoritarian and impose a new orthodoxy, frequently a very simplistic one; their lack of record keeping and overall non-systematic approach leads to great difficulties in determining accountability and effectiveness; many of them have a strong anti-professional bias that prevents a useful integration of the aprofessional and the professional approaches; they run the risk of blaming (and stigmatizing) the victim if the service fails in any way, because of their emphasis on individual responsibility rather than the social causation of problems; and finally, they have a tendency to fragment social change, as each group "does its own thing."

Filling Both Individual and Social Needs

All of these are real difficulties and must be actively guarded against if they are to be overcome or limited. Awareness, of course, is the first step, but beyond that there is a need to imitate the models that are concerned with broader social action. Direct attention will have to be given to the larger issues in our society, such as the need for national economic planning, full employment, and redistribution. As Dewar notes (1976, p. 82),

Successful self-help depends on having control over the appropriate resources, and having legal authority to act. As self-help grows in importance there will be jurisdictional fights, between professionals and self-helpers, city governments and neighborhoods, large corporations and community- or worker-controlled businesses. Some community problem solving now going on demonstrates an increasing understanding of the limits of self-help. By community problem solving, I do not mean activity that merely takes place in the community, or that defines the community as the "problem." Rather, I mean a process in which community persons and groups define the problems for themselves, identify appropriate responses to them, and directly participate in the process. Examples include efforts to gain control over urban food production and distribution; to develop locally controlled, cheap and safe energy sources; and to generate local incomes through locally owned and operated small businesses. These strategies begin with but go beyond self-help, to questions of economic and political power.

The Sidels (1976, p. 69) agree that self-help groups must begin to play a dual role, pointing out that

Medical self-help groups, for example, must not only deal with people with specific problems but must take on as their responsibility the humanizing of professionals. Community self-help groups, such as block associations, must not only provide services which are urgently needed for their blocks, but must also insist that their communities receive a just and equitable share of society's resources. Groups dealing with personal problems such as child abuse, while helping people to deal with their individual life situations, must recognize that the root of these problems lies within the broader society and take on as their responsibility the joining with other groups toward producing change in the society. Above all, all of the groups must have as part of their agenda the redistribution of wealth and power. Self-help groups must move beyond the narrow limits of dealing with the immediate problems which they were formed to face, and move toward gathering the forces, developing the methods, and providing the momentum which will lead to broader social change.

The Sidels note that the National Welfare Rights Organization (now nearly defunct) offers an example of a self-help group that both served to meet members immediate needs and was a champion of social advocacy.

Another example of a group that plays this dual role, here operating on a local and state level, is the Center for Independent Living (CIL). Organized initially by physically handicapped University of California at Berkeley students who found the university facilities and regulations unsatisfactory, CIL has grown in five years to serve some 2,000 disabled persons each month, with a staff of seventy-five (half of whom are handicapped) and an annual budget of some $900,000 (Kirschbaum, Harveston, and Katz, 1976, p. 59). Among CIL's services are counseling (mostly by peers), education, health care, housing and job placement, attendant referral, sex counseling, financial advocacy, legal assistance, and wheelchair repair. This last item typifies both the problem faced by the handicapped and CIL's approach. Because the physically handicapped are usually considered to be dependent and basically homebound, wheelchairs traditionally are not constructed to withstand outdoor use, with the consequence that among CIL's active population wheelchairs frequently break down. (Berkeley, largely as a result of CIL's pressure, has curb ramps throughout the city.) CIL both provides a twenty-four-hour repair service and is designing a new wheelchair for more active use. CIL is unique in several ways: (1) unlike most self-help groups, which are single-problem groups, CIL includes members with a multitude of handicaps—cerebral palsy, hearing impairment, multiple sclerosis, vision impairment, epilepsy, spina bifida, and other spinal chord injuries;

(2) CIL maintains a balance between the informal self-help approach and that of a large agency—CIL also provides a training program through the Center for Health Studies at Antioch College; and (3) CIL combines its service function with political and social action. This last activity has included securing civil rights of handicapped persons in obtaining a driver's license or bank account; pressuring for the removal of barriers and the enforcement of rights of access; and lobbying at the state and national levels.

Roles for the Professional

The new spreading interest in the self-help approach on the part of professional groups could lead to a positive combination of the aprofessional and the professional. However, there is also the danger that the professional will attempt to dominate and socialize the self-help groups to professional norms, coopting them and making them appendages of traditional agencies. As Antze (1976, p. 344) points out, "Whenever outsiders try to support to cooperate with one of these organizations, they run the risk of tampering with its ideology. . . . Sometimes the mere involvement of a professional can weaken the meaning of certain teachings (for example 'Only a drunk can help another drunk'). Matters become worse if the observer should point out that a given belief runs against medical knowledge, or if he counsels changes to increase the group's acceptance in professional circles. If the view developed here has been valid, then meddling of this kind would do real harm to the therapeutic process." The professional orientation, however, can also lead to concern for systematic evaluation and increased accountability. Evaluation could improve the outreach approaches of the self-help groups, so that they could attract individuals currently not drawn to them. This might be accomplished by modifying their style, approach, methods, message, program, and communication. After all, large numbers of people afflicted with various problems—from alcoholism to hypertension and diabetes—have not been drawn to self-help groups; thus, these people are left unserved, unhelped. The point is that evaluation is not to be done for some abstract general purpose, but in order to improve the functioning and reach of the organizations. Particularly pressing is the need to reach low-income populations that have been hitherto unreached. Modifying the approach and style of the self-help unit may be helpful, as may be the use of paraprofessionals from a low-income background, who could help develop links to the self-help modality.

There is also a need for a much more systematic accounting of the processes that produce the results to be evaluated—for example, there is a need for an explanation of how the self-help approach works. While we have given considerable attention in this book to presenting some possible explanatory mechanisms, it should be noted that there is no well-developed theoretical structure for most of the self-help approaches. In the mental health field, for example, the self-help movement offers no theory regarding the structure of personality or the nature of development, and in many cases it relies on fairly simplistic explanations. Again, unity with professional approaches may counteract this difficulty. Certainly the considerable research now taking place on the self-help approaches should help to systematize them and offer explanations regarding their effectiveness and power.

On the other hand, one of the major dangers that the self-help movement will face in the coming decade is precisely the fact that it may be much more closely allied with the professional and institutional structures. We have noted the positive potential in this, particularly if the unity of the aprofessional and professional modalities is to work in its best form. But while this is a worthy ideal and worth striving toward, there is no question that there will be all manner of deviations from it. In many cases, professionally led agencies will attempt to dominate and socialize self-help groups to existing professional norms. The self-help approach may then become an appendage of the professional structure, losing much of its spontaneity, vitality, innovativeness, small group character, and flexibility.

Not all professionals wish to do this, however. It is noteworthy that Gerald Caplan's Harvard group, which has quite successfully fostered the development of the Widow Program, has set a tone whereby the aprofessional self-help groups are to be independent, not to be controlled and modeled in the professional format, while at the same time providing professional support and initially actually sponsoring the development of the program. And it is not always true that the professionals coopt the self-help unit. In some cases, the self-help unit is a part of the professional structure and in other cases, as in Alcoholics Anonymous, it can facilitate cooperation among equals, that is, between the AA group and the professional organization that may refer patients to it. In other cases, the professional may assist in starting the organization, or play a monitoring back-up role. We have already noted that, with regard to low-income communities, neighborhood paraprofessionals may play an important role in bringing self-help modalities in the health and mental health and social action fields to these communities. The paraprofessional may be an important bridge between the professional organization and the self-help unit. Working formally with professional organizations can give material support and wider public and professional legitimation. "The price that formalization extracts is increased professionalization, a process which strikes at the core of self-help groups—the continual interaction among patients with mutual problems, the importance of role models, and benefits to patients themselves in the role of helping others" (Tracy and Gussow, 1976, p. 391).

Models for the Professional

There are a great variety of potential models whereby the professional relates to self-help activity. First, in the assertiveness training model, a professional psychologist typically trains a group of lay people in becoming assertive and then may train them to become trainers of others. Frequently, the women (and they are usually women) who are trained in this manner help various members of women's groups, such as consciousness-raising and support groups, to develop assertive skills. The lay trainers may return from time to time to the professionally led group for added skill training. The multiplier effect of this model is obvious: A small number of professionals have an effect that radiates out to many groups.

Second, in the peer group rap session model, there is usually one professional who trains a large number of youngsters in mutual or reciprocal counseling (sometimes called *cocounseling*) and who also plays a back-up role in the rap group meetings and in other community and school meetings in which the youngsters help other members of the community. This model is well developed in the Woodland High School in Hartsdale (reported on in Chapter Two).

Third, in the Queens College B.A. Mental Health Program, professionals train paraprofessionals in setting up various types of mutual aid groups in the community and in hospitals. The professional staff is also developing a curriculum for the training of paraprofessionals in the various skills required in setting up autonomous self-help groups. Again, as in the rap group, the multiplier effect is potentially very large.

Fourth, various health groups (discussed in Chapter Three) have been established by the American Cancer Society and other professional agencies. Here the professionals not only play a startup role, but maintain close supervision and consultation in the self-help group, as in Laryngectomy, Inc., Reach to Recovery, and the Stroke Club. In disease-specific self-help groups, dependency on treatment is an important factor in the development of the group. Some disease-specific groups depend on medical technology, as in hemophilia; other groups, such as those concerned with cystic fibrosis, rely on a combination of medicine and secondary support services.

Fifth, in the youth-tutoring-youth and children-teaching-children model in education, the professional trainer or teacher plays an important role in setting up the program, in training the participants, and in general back-up and support. Nevertheless, enormous freedom is involved—the participants develop their own curriculum for tutoring other children, meet in their own groups, discuss their problems, and develop techniques for dealing with them.

Professionals may find a sixth model in the mental health groups. In order to prevent Recovery, Inc., from being dominated by professionals, Low (its founder, and himself a mental health professional) stipulated that professionals may not hold office or become leaders of the organization (they may and sometimes do become members). In the course of its history, the organization has moved from a high level of professional supervision during its formative years to a much more independent group without professional supervision. At first the groups were located in hospitals, but the fact that doctors asked members to report to them on other members' behavior during the sessions forced the groups away from the hospitals and into the community. Nevertheless, in 1970 some 33 percent of its members came from professional referrals, a figure that has since risen to about 50 percent. In Parents Anonymous, on the other hand, a professional is typically involved in a back-up supportive and consultative role, and a professional was influential in the basic establishment of the group model. Daytop Lodge was also begun by and remains sponsored by professionals, utilizing the basic self-help approaches modeled after Synanon. And finally, many parents' groups, such as Parents of Retarded Children, have close working relationships with professionals.

Seventh, in various types of social action groups, such as tenants' organizations and welfare rights groups, professional organizers have frequently played a major role in forming the groups, catalyzing them, and assisting them in various ways, including advice, organizational training, and skill development.

Eighth, in some cases, professionals have assisted in the development of groups for hypertensive and diabetic patients. Here, the professional plays a useful disease-specific role in diagnosing the illness, in prescribing relevant drugs and regimen and in testing their effects from time to time. In addition, the professional may help such a group come together, that is, help the members to find each other, and encourage their meeting together and regulating each other. The professional or paraprofessional can provide an organizational, group-development role, sometimes utilizing the professional's prestige and medical support as a catalyst and reinforcement.

Ninth, various mutual aid groups for the aged, such as Foster Grandparents, RSVP, and Senior Companions, have been organized by professional agencies and with professional assistance. These groups, while having an attachment or connection to the back-up agency, are essentially autonomous units.

Tenth, particularly in health care, a sequential relationship between professionals and self-help groups has developed. The doctor provides the acute intervention—surgery, for example—while the self-help group takes primary responsibility for the development of adaptive behaviors.

And finally, some professionals write self-help or coping books, which large numbers of people utilize for self-help. In many cases, these people form groups in which the members help each other on the basis of the ideas and theory in the books, such as Parent Effectiveness Training, assertiveness training, reevaluative counseling, and transcendental meditation (TM). For example, a wide variety of TM groups have developed all over the country.

Thus it is clear that professionals and paraprofessionals can play a number of roles in relation to self-help groups: They may initiate such a group; they can refer persons to such a group; they can develop a group; they can consult with the group; they can staff the group, and finally, they can help the group become independent of the agency and the professional worker.

The basic issue, of course, is whether the self-help approach will be compromised through partnership with the professional sector. Without necessarily glorifying the mutual aid orientation (which is done to some extent by a number of writers), the question remains whether the self-help intervention will lose its ethos— its spirit, its populist, earthy dimension—by becoming an adjunct of the professional. In the process of revitalizing the professional approach, the mutual aid approach may lose its special character and thrust, becoming merely an arm or an adjunct of what is essentially a professionalized service. Moreover, the professional may become further removed from the client or consumer as the latter is essentially served by other consumers. In many ways, professionals may prefer this consultative, high-level, background role, having tired of direct service or having been socialized through long periods of training to a much more removed practice. These are certainly dangers to be avoided.

Also to be avoided is the danger of romanticizing the self-help approach. Sometimes self-help advocates recommend that all professional practice, in essence, imitate the self-help modality. This latter view seems to be taken by Hurvitz (1974), who, after offering a brilliant contrast between the self-help modality and the professional modality, then moves to advising the professional to imitate the self-help approach, rather than suggesting a dialectic relation where both play a positive, integrating role. Hurvitz suggests, on the basis of his comparison of psychotherapy and self-help groups, that psychotherapy should be offered without fees, records, scheduled appointments, privacy, special settings, or professional training. He also suggests that the clients should know their therapist as another human being—that the therapist should be prepared to reveal as much about himself as he asks the client to reveal.

The danger here is that what is specifically useful about the professional orientation—namely its systematic orientation, its perspective, its effort to go beyond experience—will be lost and that all practice will be *reduced* to the aprofessional dimension. Valuable as this latter dimension is, it is only part, in our view, of a broader dialectic that includes both the professional and the aprofessional. Each form of practice can benefit from some imitation of the other; the professional can become more aprofessional in some respects, identify with clients, relying more on experience, focusing on behavior changes. And the aprofessional approach certainly can lean on and utilize more theory. This is one example of the dialectic relationship between the two.

Another way of looking at the relationship between professional and aprofessional is revealed in Abrahams' (1976) analysis of types of helping relationships, based on her study of patterns of behavior of those involved in the Widowed Service Line (Abrahams, 1972), an outgrowth of the Widow-to-Widow program (Silverman, 1970, 1971, 1972). Abrahams (1976) identified a range of helper behaviors along the axis of the extent to which the helper feels the need (and is willing) to share his or her feelings with the recipient of help (see Figures 1 and 2). "The social distance maintained by the helper limits the extent to which emotional sharing is a major part of the helping style" (Abrahams, 1976, pp. 247–248). While the "Type 1" helper is what we know as "professional," one possible outcome of the relationship between the professional and the aprofessional is a new definition of *professional,* a new synthesis as a result of the dialectic process.

But it should be remembered, also, that the dialectic always includes not only the unity of opposites, but also the *struggle* of opposites, and thus the continuing battle between the professional and aprofessional is useful, with each side demonstrating its own value and criticizing some of the limitations of the other approach.

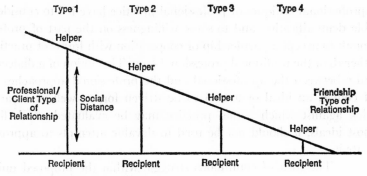

Source: Abrahams (1976, p. 248).

Figure 1. Helping relationships along the continuum from professional/client to friendship type of relationship.

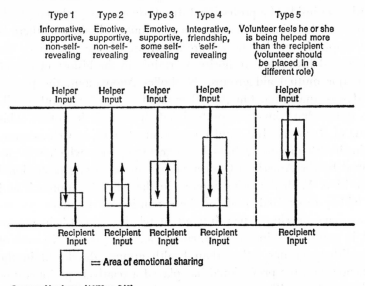

Source: Abrahams (1976, p. 248).

Figure 2. Sharing feelings in the mutual help relationship.

Aprofessional critiques of professional practice have led to considerable demystification and to some willingness on the part of professionals to accept a partnership or cooperation with forms of practice other than the traditional professional ones. The notion of a dialectic unity between the aprofessional and the professional approaches is, of course, an ideal or a goal to be striven for, as well as a yardstick against which actual practice may be evaluated—and, like most ideals, it should not be used to devalue attempts to approximate it.

The idea of continuous struggle within the proposed unity indicates a basic contradiction in the idea of relating the professional to the self-help mutual aid structure. At one level, at least, the self-help movement is deeply antiprofessional, certainly in its ethos and pretty much so in its operation, because it arose in part because of the deficiencies of the professional and the professionalized institutions. Furthermore, the self-help unit often arises autonomously, not inside of a professional structure or agency; the emphasis is on people serving each other on a voluntary basis, and there is little emphasis on the special presumed knowledge that gives the professional his or her authority. Certainly in the history of one of the major mutual aid groups, Alcoholics Anonymous, the professional was anathema. On the other hand, a number of other self-help groups have involved professionals from their inception. This is true of Recovery, Inc., and Parents Anonymous, as well as many of the health groups such as Laryngectomy, Inc., which was developed by the American Cancer Society under strong professional supervision. With the rising interest in the self-help approach and the widely recognized need for the expansion of resources, professionals have developed new interest in relating to self-help groups and, in many cases, in starting them or catalyzing them.* In most of the self-help groups, other than health groups, developed in the past, however, the professional has played a relatively peripheral or background role. The paramount question of the future is whether professionals will play a much more predominant, perhaps even coopting role, as they relate more fully to the self-help modality.

Self-help groups are in many instances permitting professionals to "cop out," to avoid the more difficult caring aspects of

* At least two schools of social work, Smith College and Case Western Reserve University, are offering courses in self-help.

their professional role and to focus increasingly on its less threatening, more technological aspects. Professionals must not be permitted to evade their responsibilities for human care. The surgeon, for example, must be as concerned about the emotional aspects of the loss of a breast as he or she is about the technical aspects of the spread of the cancer or the nature of the surgery. Self-help groups, since they cannot replace the professional expertise needed in many of the technical aspects of medical care, must not encourage the abdication by the technical expert of concern in the area of caring as well. Self-help groups must be as concerned about teaching professionals how to work humanely with patients or clients as with helping the people directly to help themselves (Sidel and Sidel, 1976). The professional must be viewed as a servant of the society and must be reeducated to play that role. Professionals must be required to learn from the nonhierarchical characteristics of the self-help movement new ways of relating to patients and to one another. Relieving professionals of responsibility for caring roles or unnecessarily driving them away from self-help groups will not help accomplish these goals.

The experience of CanCervive, a project of the Los Angeles chapter of the American Cancer Society that sought to use self-help approaches (Kleiman, Mantel, and Alexander, 1976), illustrates the problems likely to occur when professional providers and self-help modalities combine. Basically, the program was an effort to use cancer patients with uncertain prognoses in a visitor program; previously, only recovered cancer patients were used. Almost everything that could go wrong did, largely as a consequence of the tension between the lay approach put forth by the cancer patients who wanted to act and the norms and procedures of the Cancer Society.

The failure of CanCervive seems to have been more than a result of staff blunders. To a considerable extent, it appears that a fundamentally differing set of values, beliefs, and behaviors separated the volunteers and the professionals. "A major cohesive force in self-help groups is the egalitarian belief that all members are capable of counseling. Yet the professionals evaluated the volunteers according to their own criteria and assigned patients to those they saw as more skilled. The interjection of a hierarchical structure, with its inevitable jealousy and rivalry, effectively destroyed much of the supportive, peer group atmosphere" (Kleiman, Mantel, and Alexander, 1976, p. 409).

It is a comment as to the limits of the data available that this case study is the only one of its type. Without additional information about CanCervive, as well as case studies of other relationships between professional organizations and self-help, it is impossible to reach any final conclusions as to the meaning of the illustration. However, the study does make yet clearer the complexities and complications involved.

Techniques Are Not Socially and Politically Neutral

Techniques or approaches such as self-help, of course, are not neutral. They can be used counter to the presumed good intentions of their designers or their potential. Barbara Ehrenreich (1974, p. 56) makes this point in regard to women's self-help:

> Take two popular forms of women's self-help—gynecological self-help and Weight Watchers. I'm convinced that gynecological self-help effectively subverts the social control functions of conventional women's medical services. The recipient (participant) is freed from medical mystifications about her own body and learns that she is empowered to face the conventional providers (which she must, because self-help is a long way from embracing comprehensive care), in an active, questioning stance.
>
> On the other hand, Weight Watchers seems to me to be a clear-cut case of enlisting women in their own oppression. The great majority of Weight Watchers are not pathologically obese women, but ordinary women who are striving desperately to fit into socially determined norms of feminine beauty. The prime Weight Watcher tactics—ridicule and humiliation—are superbly designed to enforce the notions that (1) the "Overweight" woman is despicable and unsexy, and (2) that all women are self-indulgent, childlike creatures. It is indeed correct that a particular mode or technique constrains against or conduces toward a particular direction, and what is necessary to do is to abet that tendency (or to fight against it, as necessary).

In a sense, all forms of service delivery have aspects of social control, implicit and explicit. One must assess, then, what happens to the social control function of a particular service when there is a switch from a provider-dominated to a more consumer-intensive self-help mode of delivery. One possibility may be that the self-help delivery mode simply provides a more appealing package for a service that is not "selling well" in the provider-dominated mode. For example, youth-tutoring-youth programs could become a more efficient and attractive way of selling the ideological content of public education to otherwise recalcitrant target groups, such as ghetto youth. In this case, the more self-help mode could be seen as a stratagem for enlisting the oppressed in their own oppression.

On the other hand, the self-help mode may fundamentally alter and even subvert the social control functions of the service. To take youth-tutoring-youth again: This kind of participation in service production may empower youth to such an extent that many of the oppressive ideological messages of education are negated. On another level, it may lead the student participants to challenge the tracking, grading, and hierarchy that now characterize the school system.

We believe that the consumer-intensive self-help design does conduce in general toward a fuller and more self-determining role for the consumer; that it encourages both greater effectiveness for the consumer; and, when carried out in concert with consumer participation in governance, that this effectiveness will more likely be consumer determined and consumer benefiting. None of this is guaranteed. All of this requires struggle, and all of it is continuingly in question.

In the self-help mode, the consumer who is also a producer is more involved in the very shaping of the service, is nearer to it, and is likely to be more knowledgable about it. This combination may affect the entire fabric of accountability. It can be hypothesized that a self-help mode may encourage greater accountability to the consumer, as contrasted to more traditional service modes, in which accountability is more likely to be addressed toward the agency hierarchy, the taxpayer, and the services' "owners."

Self-Help and Bureaucracy

The involvement of the consumer in the double role of both consumer and producer may discourage hierarchical and bureaucratic modes of organization. The self-help approach dovetails with the modern critique of bureaucracy. A major criticism of bureaucratic organization is that it does not primarily serve the client, but rather serves the bureaucratic system itself, in the process producing perhaps some internal efficiency (although it has dysfunctions here as well). The basic thrust of the self-help approach is deeply anti-bureaucratic and antihierarchical, because self-help rests on the assumption that the efficiency of the system comes at the point of relationship between the consumer and server, not within the service system itself, unless the changes in the latter are fundamentally related to the consumer.

A key question concerns the type of relationship that will exist between the professional agency and the self-help group. Will the professional attempt to dominate and socialize the self-help group to existing professional norms, or will the self-help group be independent, have a cooperative relationship with the professional structure, and thereby significantly modify a basic dependency relationship in our society?

It is our hope and belief that the self-help movement represents a new dynamism in human service practice—a force that is likely to lead to new forms of strength-based practice (built on what a person can actually do); to more spontaneity and flexibility; to less bureaucracy, less adherance to traditional outmoded approaches; and to more innovative, people-serving, consumer-based methods. It is a force for change that now plays a somewhat similar role to that of the paraprofessional movement of the 1960s. As the self-help movement becomes absorbed and institutionalized, it will necessarily lose some of that force and character, but in doing so, it may change the traditional institutional forms, and improve the human service system, its productivity and effectiveness. This is part of the cycle of change, where the new loses its newness as it changes the old. Then, as we move on, we must look to new forces and new dimensions, perhaps not yet perceivable, that will operate as the dynamism in the next period. Unless we understand this dimension of institutional change, we may become discouraged and pessimistic as the new spontaneous, strength-based orientation loses some of that character, as it becomes part of the old and, in turn, becomes tradition.

The Social Context of Self-Help

Most of our attention in this book has been directed at human service mutual aid approaches. We have noted some of the factors accounting for the rapid growth and spread of these approaches: the high cost of professional services, the critique of professionalism, an aging population that has a high incidence of chronic illnesses that are particularly amenable to self-help interventions. In order to shed further light on the whole self-help ethos, it may be useful now to examine one of its manifestations that we have not attended to, namely the extensive proliferation of various types of grassroots mutual aid groups—block associations, tenants associations, groups concerned with various types of local direct action aimed at lowering utility rates, halting the construction of highways that would destroy neighborhoods, obtaining free bus service for senior citizens, opposing discriminatory hiring and promotion practices for women, and preventing redlining (in which banks refuse to make loans to entire neighborhoods).

Perlman (1976) visited over sixty grassroots groups in sixteen states and developed a threefold typology to describe them: (1) direct action groups that pressure existing authorities for accountability and specific policy outputs; (2) electoral groups that attempt to become the existing authorities; and (3) alternative institution groups that bypass the existing authorities (such as community development corporations, cooperatives, and self-help enterprises). Alvin Toffler also describes a variety of "anticipatory democracy" self-help groups developing throughout the country (particularly in the states of Washington and Hawaii), in which people come together to make plans about local policies.

These groups seem to be characterized by a great need to be able to affect something at some level, to feel some degree of control and influence. Moreover, they like action. There is a lot of doing, not just thinking. There is little concern about dealing with big things and changing the world; in fact, there is a retreat and sometimes a disavowal of that type of emphasis. Antibigness, antihierarchy, and anticorporateness are important dimensions of these groups. They are essentially centered on the consumer, rather than on the producer or worker. They are concerned with the problems of living as experienced by the consumer in everyday life.

They fasten on a great variety of consumer issues including the environment, housing, women's issues, local services, prices, and taxes. The organizations, when they arise, are fairly loose and often not enduring. Their methods include boycotts, demonstrations, consciousness-raising approaches, media-oriented activity, and legal action. The groups are generally unconnected with each other; at best they form loose networks and sometimes movements, such as the welfare rights movement of the 1960s, the environmental movement, and the women's movement. This tendency is in contrast to organizations with clear structures, such as trade unions or political parties. The groups are diverse and fragmented, but they are involving and contagious, often making decisions through consensus rather than formal democratic processes.

All of these groups have to varying degrees been affected by much of the 1960s' ethos: the interpersonal, cultural, and sexual revolutions; the concern for the quality of life and work; the affective orientation; the new humanism; the antimaterialist, antiacquisitive, antiindustrialist forces; the emphasis on individualism and alternative ways of doing things, on self-expression, self-actualization, personal liberation, autonomy, identity, self-determination, the relevance; "now" orientation; the antitechnocratic, antipragamatic, egalitarian, antihierarchical themes; and the emphasis on advocacy, anticonformity, and antitradition. These are the themes of an expanding, consumer-oriented society heavily influenced by nonworking populations or by working populations in their consumer roles. After all, it was not women workers who led the development of the women's movement, or young workers who sparked the students' movements, or any kind of workers who developed the welfare rights movement. Rather, these movements were generated by people in their consumer roles, some of whom had been removed from the work force temporarily or permanently, others whose affluence (freedom from insecurity) enabled them to be concerned with questions such as the environment and the quality of life. While the values and issues that these groups raise may have spread to other segments of the population, the initial thrust seems clearly to have been coming from groups not integrated into worker roles.

Perlman (1976) argues that the present social and political struggles are not at the "point of production," as the neo-Marxists might claim, but rather at the point of consumption, particularly because the union movement in the United States, with few exceptions, is relatively conservative, and because there is no major political party, in her view, that represents any strong critique of the society. "Progressive struggles at the point of consumption however, are abundant in the United States, as in many countries in the advanced stages of capitalism. Community-based groups which organize around economistic demands, end up raising consciousness in the process. They are a logical outgrowth of the expanding role of the state, the growing importance of the indirect wage, and the increasing collective nature of the consumption of municipal services. The lines of conflict become drawn then more and more between the individuals and the state, or some part of its regulatory apparatus, rather than between the individuals and their employer" (Perlman, 1976, p. 20).

In an earlier work (Gartner and Riessman, 1974), we theorized that *consumers* are becoming a central force in the emerging service society for the following reasons:

1. They are needed in the market to buy the overproduced goods.
2. They are encouraged to be continuously dissatisfied with last year's products.
3. They are "exploited" via high prices and taxes.
4. They have free time in which to engage with each other and to consider their dissatisfactions and common interests.
5. They are less socialized by the traditional industrial workplace.
6. Finally, certain consumer groups—minorities, women, and youth—are doubly alienated and angered because they are discriminated against by racism, sexism, and adultism and restricted from access to the industrial setting and the body politic.

In a way, the backlash of the 1970s against the progressive, expansionary 1960s seems to have led the larger movements that arose in the earlier period to go more local, to emphasize more than ever the local base, the community, with the concomitant feeling that efforts at the big national level are impossible or when they are temporarily achieved they soon are coopted and destroyed. Thus, in the 1970s we have fewer large national movements, but much more local activity, largely unsung, unheard of, and undramatic.

Then, too, much of the current activity involves a more educated citizenry, including many more affluent middle-class people and others who have considerable leisure time and who have been prepared by their education and media-induced awareness not to accept passivity, to want to have some control over their lives and the processes affecting these lives. Feeling that it is impossible to do so at the larger national level, there has been what might be called a *retreat* (depending on one's point of view) to the local agenda, where one's efforts may bear fruit.*

Perlman (1976, p. 19) sums up the issue with regard to grassroots self-help groups:

Both the pitfalls and the potentials are great. The key questions are: (1) whether these groups will be able to sustain the motivation and mobilization of their membership; (2) whether they will be able to overcome the limits of their localism and take on larger-scale issues and struggles; (3) whether they will survive the inevitable attempts at cooptation and/or repression once they begin to pose more of a threat to established interests; (4) whether they can unite to forge a national federation of grassroots groups; (5) whether they will begin to develop political consciousness and ideological clarity; (6) whether they will be able to build alliances with labor; and finally (7) whether they contain the seeds of a new radical party of a movement to transform the Democratic Party. Whatever the future may hold, people are coming to understand the issues and identify the enemy, are learning to fight strategically on their own behalf, and are gaining confidence in their collective abilities.

Conclusion

It is clear that there are many dangers in the self-help thrust: victim blaming, fragmentation, symptom treatment rather

***

* No doubt the regionalism and ethnic diversity of the United States contributes further to the localism characteristic of the self-help approach.

than structural change, and so on. Still, there are important models where the mutual aid unit is integrated or connected in some way with larger social movements that are directed toward major social change. This has been true of the women's movement, the welfare rights movement, and the movement of the handicapped. Here the smaller self-help microcosm is an essential feature of the larger thrust. This chapter also has presented possible roles for the professional in relation to the self-help modality, while recognizing the difficulties and the tensions.

❧❧❧❧ 6 ❧❧❧❧

Conclusion:
New Directions
for Self-Help Groups

❧❧❧❧❧❧❧❧❧❧❧❧❧❧❧❧

The rapid proliferation of self-help groups not only reflects the decline of traditional integrating institutions such as the family, the church, and the neighborhood, but it also reflects the inadequacy of the formal caregiving institutions in meeting needs that arise in the absence of these bonding structures. The self-help world view seems particularly responsive to the new problems coming to the fore, such as the character problems associated with drug addiction, alcoholism, and child abuse; the highly resistant health-related behaviors, such as smoking and overeating; and the chronic health problems associated with an aging population. Many of the mental health problems also have a chronic character, and so the usual episodic forms of mental health intervention may be less appropriate

147

than the continuous, all-embracing interventions of the mutual aid form.

Mutual aid is also indicated for the general problems of living. Modern problems do not necessarily take the form of a specific disorder, such as alcoholism, but in many cases are more diffuse problems of living, such as are experienced by many women and men in consciousness-raising groups, by the large number of people who use the coping books, and by members of the various encounter groups. Then there are the problems of specific groups such as parents of retarded children, exoffenders, parents without partners, people who are dying, the identity problems of the young, special problems of older people, and the unique problems of midgets.

Finally, there are the problems related to social action and social change reflected in the 1960s in the welfare rights movement and, more currently, in the block associations, food cooperatives, energy-conserving groups, and housing self-management associations. These groups reflect a gap in our society—a political alienation gap. They are opting for more decentralized, local forms of action.

There is no question that no matter what the limitations of the self-help mode may be, this is where the action is—where real people are responding to the new problems of today's society in the only way that they know how—in small, autonomous, cooperative groups. Such groups are the grassroots response to modern nihilism, pessimism, hopelessness, cynicism, and feelings of powerlessness. Thus it is very important to understand and to study in order to learn from them, to see what direction they may take, and to see what their relationship may be to the large, formal institutional structure.

Self-help groups are important because of the resources (human and financial) they marshall and the power they wield, as well as because of the ways in which they influence the public attitude in relation to particular services. At the same time, while it may be accurate to state, as do Levin, Katz, and Holst (1976), that some 85 percent of health care is self-care, nonetheless, when people consider health they think of doctors and other providers in the formal health care system. Thus, a central concern must be how self-help affects the major institutional forms in health, mental health, education, social welfare, rehabilitation, and recreation.

Two Facets of Self-Help

The significance of the mutual aid movement can be seen from two perspectives: (1) the ways in which the self-help approach relates to the character and quality of human service practice, and (2) the relevance of the mutual aid world view to social and political change.

Human Services Practice. Much of human service practice in the self-help area has been directed toward a middle-class clientele. It is widely believed that the self-help mutual aid movement typically fails to attract low-income members, that it is largely a middle-class movement. Certainly, this appears to be true for many of the traditional mental health-oriented groups, such as Recovery, Inc., and historically is probably true of Alcoholics Anonymous and most of the other "anonymous" groups. But perhaps a more careful analysis is needed. It may very well be that a careful systematic analysis of the way self-help groups function might lead to suggestions for modification that would enlist and hold low-income clients.

Low-income groups in the United States have expressed their interest in self-help in a great variety of ways: in the Home-Town clubs of Puerto Ricans living on the mainland; in block associations and tenants' groups; in anticrime groups and safety patrols; in groups such as the Sisterhood of Black Single Mothers; in organizations such as Fightback!, which includes unemployed persons who rehabilitate housing for themselves and members of their community; in welfare rights groups; in veterans groups, in youth groups and gangs such as Chicago's Blackstone Rangers; in exoffender groups such as the Fortune Society; in storefront churches; in informal, shared child-care groupings; and in "rap groups." Moreover, children in low-income communities learn extremely well by teaching other children (in fact, the successful youth-tutoring-youth designs were originally developed among the poor during the 1960s' antipoverty program)'. Not all these examples match the more classical definitions of mutual aid, but in many cases they have much in common with those definitions.

The point, of course, can be made that low-income populations seem to be drawn more to social action and neighborhood and ethnic support groups, rather than to the more mental health and health relevant groups. But is it true that the low-income populations do not have these other problems? One might ask, does alcoholism not prevail in low-income communities? Is drug addiction not a concern among the poor? Are hypertension and diabetes not problems among the black community? Is mental illness a middle-class phenomenon? Are there no battered wives among the poor? Are the families of alcoholics in low-income communities comfortable? Are there no lonely parents without partners in working-class and low-income communities?

Perhaps these problems need to be met via the development of *new forms and new styles of mutual aid*. Groups in the human service areas, such as Alcoholics Anonymous, might be much more effective in reaching the low-income populations if they added a social dimension and were less narrow in their appeal and function. At this stage, this is merely a hypothesis requiring much more research for confirmation. But the implications for the self-help movement are enormous. It could be greatly expanded if it could reach low-income populations by modifications of its style and appeal, and large numbers of severely underserved communities would thereby be served. This is just one area where research may be very valuable for the self-help movement itself.

The involvement of low-income groups in the self-help social movement has other broad implication; these groups are far more oriented toward social action and perhaps, social change, and this has great importance for the dilemma of the radical perspective, to be discussed later in this chapter.

Systematic study also could help to clarify the helping processes and mechanisms that are utilized in the mutual aid groups. And consciousness of these processes and mechanisms could improve the training and preparation of members of the groups and thus also improve practice.

At one level, it can be argued that the self-help groups by

their very essence are nonprofessional and that any professional involvement might contaminate them in a variety of ways. They might attempt to imitate professional practice; they may be coopted by the professionals, or dominated by them; they might lose their purity, their simplicity, and their closeness to the people and the problems. Some have contended that researching these groups interferes with their functioning and their helping behaviors. Why not leave them alone? After all, the professionals have not done such a good job, and researching professional practice has not always been clearly beneficial. The mutual aid groups seem to be helping people: their members achieve satisfaction. Might not all this be lost through professional intervention?

We have constantly stressed the need for integration of the professional and aprofessional—that each has a role to play and that the aprofessional self-help orientation need not be seen as competitive or even alternative to the professional perspective. There is reason to believe that self-help approaches might benefit professional practice. Some integration is beginning to take place because of professionals' failure and because of the feeling of a need for improvement. Moreover, the self-help groups also might benefit. The fact is that many of them, such as Parents Anonymous, have reached out for professional assistance, and, as we have indicated throughout this book, many have been initiated by professional agencies, such as the American Cancer Society.

As Dewar (1976) notes, there are essentially two kinds of help—personal and technical. Personal help, by which he means human comfort, support, reassurance, and mutual caring, is particularly dealt with through the mutual aid modality. Technical help, which includes expert information, skill, and tools, is more often the province of the professional. Dewar points out that it is impossible to "deliver" personal help, "for you can't really produce, consume, or deliver personal help. Personal help is based on mutuality, similarity of participant, and their viewpoints and self-defined problems. On the other hand, technical help is unilateral, based on differences between participants and directed by externally defined problems, and externally controlled resources" (Dewar, 1976, p. 80).

Social Change. From the perspective of social change, the

self-help approach offers some contradictory tendencies. On the one hand, the entire ethos of the movement is generally critical of traditional institutions, although the depth of this criticism varies from the women's consciousness-raising groups on the one hand to those less interested in social change, such as the various "anonymous" groups, on the other hand. But whether directly concerned with major societal transformation or not, the thrust of the movement is critical of much of human service practice, professional behavior, and institutional arrangements.

However, the basic character of the movement is locally directed, focused on specific problem areas such as drug addiction; moreover, there is little linking of the essentially fragmented network of self-help groups. So each does its own thing with its own agenda. Sometimes the agenda moves from local to national organization, as in AA or the Parents of Retarded Children, but even then the program is geared to a narrow interest sphere, rather than to the kinds of structural proposals that would be necessary for radical societal reorganization. The groups might coalesce and actually move in this direction, but the tendency is to function in what might be called a *consumerist* fashion, that is, to organize around specific consumer interests rather than changing the producer or the basic institutional system (Creighton, 1976).

There may be spin-offs or by-products from the practice of the self-helpers that do affect larger national systems, such as national health insurance (if it is to come), but this link is almost fortuitous. At the present time, self-help practice remains marginal, compared to these larger systems. It is essentially on the periphery, largely functioning to help its own members survive in a negative environment. To some extent, the women's movement is an exception, but recent data indicate that the consciousness-raising unit is increasingly moving away from a political perspective and much more to an interpersonal one (Lieberman and Bond, 1976). To what degree the women's consciousness-raising groups mesh with (or articulate with) the larger national feminist movement is at this time unclear. The National Welfare Rights Organization, a highly significant low-income-oriented group with a mutual aid base and a national organization, has not survived the 1960s very well.

Aside from the question of affecting large, human service institutional arenas, there is the question of the way in which mutual aid groups formulate the problems with which they deal. The major problems of our time relate fundamentally to the distribution and direction of resources, jobs, inflation, social and economic planning, and social class issues. Unless attention is directed forcefully to these questions, it may well be that the self-help movement will deal with social symptoms at best, on a fragmentary, single-issue basis, rather than with the major *big* causes of the local problems that flow from the national level. Job creation and inflation are not problems that can be solved at the local level by mutual support groups, nor are the distribution and organization of energy, or the tax base. How much of our resources is spent on military expenditures, rather than on people, is not directly determinable by the mutual aid format or strategy. Changing our society will require the organization of stable, large-scale political power bases and political organization, with an action program that cuts across the more phenotypic issues of gambling compulsion, drug addiction, and the like.

For the most part, the self-help approach does not look to structural societal solutions. Thus, AA is concerned about the treatment of the alcoholic, not about the removal of alcohol or the societally produced stresses related to the stimulation of drinking. Similarly the antidrug self-help groups are largely concerned with rehabilitating the addict, rather than with treating the causes of addiction. Some self-help groups, of course, are more socially oriented. Certainly this is true of the exoffenders and the handicapped groups. But there is a basic tendency in the self-help world view to (1) deal with the problem at the symptom level; (2) look for small-scale solutions; (3) define marginal alternatives to the major institutional caregiver system; and (4) be broadly critical of institutions and the societal framework, but not to organize a direct, rounded political attack.

Nevertheless, their basic ethos and dealienating potential contribute in a nonspecific, indirect fashion to social criticism and, perhaps, to social action. If these feelings and new consciousness can be organized, or in some way connected to more politically oriented movements or coalitions, then the self-help thrust may make a contribution to societal change. The problem remains, however, that the self-help orientation allows for retreat from the larger agenda. Many self-helpers feel nothing can be accomplished at the larger system level, and all that can be done is at the smaller level, either in the family or small group, or for oneself, in an extreme privatism—"I can't affect big government, I can only affect small me, or a me that is extended to like me's, who are in the same boat."

While the self-helpers provide mutual support, share problems and cope at some level, the large-scale difficulties remain. There are not enough jobs, basic services are severely inadequate, inflation continues, the poor remain poor, discrimination, sexism and racism flourish, there is no redistribution, and a large proportion of our taxes is used for the military. To this, the self-help group member says, "All these basic difficulties continue to affect me and my local group, but I survive as best I can by essentially ignoring the big items and concentrating on the little things that I can do." This is the dilemma, and the resolution of the dilemma cannot remain within the framework of the political consciousness of the self-help movement. That movement must be penetrated by and affected by political ideology and understanding deriving from an analysis at the larger national level.

The extreme political perspective of some of the self-helpers, which seems to argue that the system will fall of its own weight if we do not participate in it, if we do not vote, if we deschool, if we provide all our health care through self-care, represents (in our view) simplistic retreatism. We think it is unlikely that the system will be transformed in this fashion, and, even if it were to fall, the anarchy that would replace it by no means guarantees a progressive radical future. Perhaps a more interesting model to explore is the relationship in Italy, between the local left organizations and their control of cities like Bologna and the larger national agenda of the left parties. Here, both groups are highly conscious about the need for molar social and economic change, including national economic planning directed at dealing with the fundamental problems of the society. What occurs at the local level is the attempt in miniature or in microcosm to produce as *far as possible* (recognizing that this is limited by the larger framework) some of the social character and quality that might inhere in the whole society if the major social changes could be made. But the larger ideological socialist consciousness is attached to both levels, and the local organizations are quite aware that they are working toward socialist ends.

It is possible to see the self-help groups coalescing into a movement or at least into a strong network directed toward some common objectives. They could come together because of similar aims or common enemies. However, this seems very unlikely, largely because these groups have such widely different goals and constituencies, to say nothing of the fact that their basic orientation is essentially localistic. Self-help groups have retreated from the larger national issues and have focused instead on problems that they feel they can affect. Therefore, it seems highly improbable that they would ally to form a national movement. However, the notion of such a coalition is only one model of social change. It may well be that the grassroots mutual aid groups may contribute to social change via a very different route.

It is our hypothesis that the self-help approach can contribute significantly to social change by reducing alienation and increasing empowerment. In attempting to achieve some measure of control in areas close to their lives, in their communities and neighborhoods, rather than in the national arena, where they feel powerless, people have reached out to form all types of mutual aid groups, from block associations to women's consciousness-raising groups. In these groups, they feel a sense of power; here they can achieve something. This may contribute to their dealienation and even their empowerment.

To accomplish this, it is not necessary that the local groups become national movements; they may not coalesce, or unite; they may not lead people to move from the smaller local agendas to the larger national picture in and of themselves. But, insofar as they reduce alienation, they may remove at the psychological level what in the 1970s has become a major interference to large-scale political action in America, namely, the feeling of powerlessness. This psychological state, the very opposite of that which existed in the 1960s, leads to lack of participation in the larger political processes, at the polls, at conventions, in primaries, and in building political organizations. If the grassroots mutual aid activity does nothing more than contribute to the reduction of the interfering alienation, it will have accomplished a great deal.

A Balance Sheet

What, then, have we learned from these mutual help groups that may have broad meaning and value? Assuming a degree of effectiveness or at least an appeal to increasing segments of the population, what principles guide the self-help intervention, either implicitly or explicitly?

Mutual aid groups appear to integrate a great variety of approaches to behavior change, derived from multiple levels of experience. Some utilize traditional principles based on will, inspiration, and the demand for action and motion. They all use the principles of group reinforcement and group support; they all demand reciprocity and mutual helping; they seem to be rooted in role theory and behavioristic models (they ask that the group member behave "as if" he or she were well, or nonalcoholic, or emotionally integrated); they are strength-based (they call upon the coping abilities and the strengths of the individual to overcome the pathology, the crisis, the problem); they use simple principles or persuasion ideologies, such as the AA's Twelve Steps, that tend to demystify complicated mechanisms; they provide corrective emotional experiences, through the group and through cooperation, mutuality, and helping; they are not episodic—they are continuous, fill time, and structure the day; they emphasize socialization and commitment, rather than formal training; they provide models— the oldtimer, the helper; they fight relapse or regression; they diffuse and share leadership; they use their own resources or skills, the resources of the consumer; and they attempt to build a new way of life, a subculture, a community, a movement. Sometimes they develop a special mechanism such as the Synanon Game, where they aim for gut honesty, ripping away the shreds of social deception, building candor, intimacy and expressiveness, recapturing existential values of unity and belonging and attempting to root out the ill effects of bureaucratic relationships and impersonal authority.

In essence, then, the mutual help groups combine a great

variety of sociological and psychological principles involved in changing behavior. They typically are not concerned with exploring childhood causes. Their emphasis is on present behavior—in some cases, symptoms—but most of them are concerned not only with reducing or controlling symptoms, but also with building positive mental health, integrated human relations, honesty, and the like.

At a more complex level, Synanon, with its total environment and total leader, dialectically polarizes the characteristics of safety, security, organization, stability, leadership, and authority, on the one hand, in the "triangle," that is, in the everyday life of the community, while the "circle," the Synanon Game, accents the reverse— complete equality, no authority, open expression of all feelings, anarchy, no concern with politeness, irreverence, and nondiscipline. This balance or dialectic polarization may provide a unique and important contribution to understanding deep behavioral change.

There is clearly a need for much more study of self-help modalities and practices, as there are hardly any controlled, careful studies to verify the effectiveness of these groups (Lieberman and Borman, 1976a). The evidence for the most part is suggestive (although also sometimes persuasive), anecdotal, and impressionistic. We do not know whether the self-help approaches apply only to special segments of the population or help with special problems. We usually do not know whether the reported results reflect consumer satisfaction—a major benefit in itself—rather than objectively measured behavioral change. It is useful to know, for example, that weight-reducing self-help groups are as effective as professionalized medical diets (Stunkard, 1972), but often the effects of neither last too long.

We need much more information about the way the self-help approaches work, with what populations, and for how long. We need to know how objectively and how subjectively effective they are. The self-help groups themselves need to become deeply involved in this evaluative process, but they also need the help of professional social scientists and evaluators, as well as of theorists who will help codify the principles and methods that are employed. This help is important, because it may be necessary in some cases to modify the self-help model in order to appeal to populations hitherto unreached. This understanding and evaluation is critical, moreover, if self-help practice is to affect the major formal caregiving institutions of our society that badly need to be improved.

Finally, it is important to note the dangers of the mutual aid approach: It may substitute self-help for system change—that is, it may reduce the responsibility of the system; it may fragment the forces working toward change; it may foster privatism—turning people inward, diverting them from social causation and social action; it may impose a middle-class self-help mode on low-income populations; it may be coopted by professionals and their agencies; it may foster dependence, it may impose new authoritarian orthodoxies; it may constrain against systematic evaluation; it may provoke strong antiprofessional biases preventing a useful integration of the aprofessional and the professional approaches; and it may stigmatize and blame the victim. Moreover, it may enhance the romantic belief that small group approaches are the essence of social change, that small alone is beautiful, and that decentralization is the only way to change society. These dangers need not become realities, provided the self-help approach is not viewed as a cure-all for our deep societal problems, but rather as one element in a strategy directed toward large-scale ideologically based structural change.

Appendix A

Directory of
Self-Help Groups

≋≋≋≋≋≋≋≋≋≋≋≋≋≋≋≋

We have prepared this list to assist persons wishing to contact self-help groups. Where possible, the address we have listed is the organization's national office; most of them will provide a list of their member groups. It has been our experience that people in self-help groups are very generous in their willingness to share information and to be of assistance to others in need.

In addition to the groups themselves, assistance can be provided by The National Self-Help Clearinghouse, 184 Fifth Avenue, New York City, NY 10010. It offers a variety of services, as well as publishing reports, papers, and a newsletter.

Abused Women's Aid in Crisis
GPO Box 1699
New York, NY 10010
For battered wives and other abused women.

Addicts Anonymous
Box 2000
Lexington, KY 41991
For drug addicts.

Al-Anon
P.O. Box 182
Madison Square Station
New York, NY 10010
For families of alcoholics.

Alateen
200 Park Avenue South
New York, NY 10003
For teenage children of alcoholics.

Alcoholics Anonymous
AA World Services
P.O. Box 459
Grand Central Station
New York, NY 10017
For adult alcoholics.

Alexander Graham Bell Association for the Deaf
3417 Volta Place, N.W.
Washington, DC 20007
For deaf persons.

American Blind Bowling Association
5338 Queensbridge Road
Madison, WI 53714
Bowling for blind persons.

American Diabetes Association
18 East 48th Street
New York, NY 10017
For diabetics, youth and adult, and their families.

American Federation of Catholic Workers for the
    Blind and Visually Handicapped
154 East 23rd Street
New York, NY 10010
For blind persons of the Catholic faith.

American Schizophrenia Association
Huxley Institute
1114 First Avenue
New York, NY 10021
>*For adult schizophrenics.*

Arthritis Federation
1212 Avenue of the Americas
New York, NY 10036
>*For arthritics, youth and adult, and their families.*

Arthritis Foundation
475 Riverside Drive
New York, NY 10027
>*For arthritics, youth and adult, and their families.*

Associated Blind
135 West 23rd Street
New York, NY 10010
>*For blind persons.*

Associated Rational Thinkers
117 West Main Street
Madison, WI 53703
>*A mental health support group.*

Association for Advancement of Blind Children
162–10 Highland Avenue
Jamaica, NY 11432
>*For blind children and their parents.*

Association for Children with
    Learning Disabilities
5225 Grace Street
Pittsburgh, PA 15236
>*For children with learning disabilities and their parents.*

Association for Children with Retarded
    Mental Development
902 Broadway
New York, NY 10010
>*For mentally retarded children and their parents.*

Association for the Education of the
       Visually Handicapped
1604 Spruce Street
Philadelphia, PA 19103
       For visually handicapped persons.

Asthmatic Children Foundation of New York
333 East 69th Street
New York, NY 10021
       For asthmatic children and their parents.

Athletics for the Blind
41 West 33rd Street
New York, NY 10001
       For blind adults.

Black Lung Association
1222 Washington Street, East
Charleston, WV 25301
       For miners with black lung disease and their families.

Blinded Veterans Association
1735 De-Sales Street, N.W.
Washington, DC 20036
       For blind veterans and their families.

Buxom Belles International
20515 Westover
Southfield, MI 48075
       For overweight women.

Calix Society
21 Southeast Prince
Minneapolis, MN 55414
       *For the spiritual needs of alcoholics of the Catholic faith;
       most members have also joined AA.*

Candlelighters
123 C Street, S.E.
Washington, DC 20003
       For parents of children with cancer.

Center for Independent Living
2539 Telegraph Avenue
Berkeley, CA 94704
> *For handicapped persons and their families.*

Checks Anonymous
Box 81248
Lincoln, NB 68501
> *For persons in debt.*

Children's Hearing Education and Research
871 MacLean Avenue
Yonkers, NY 10704
> *For hard of hearing children and their families.*

Committee to Combat Huntington's Disease
250 West 57th Street
Suite 2016
New York, NY 10019
> *For persons with Huntington's disease and their families.*

Congress of People with Disabilities
170 Broadway
New York, NY 10038
> *For handicapped persons and their families.*

Cooley's Anemia Blood and Research Foundation
    for Children
3366 Hillside Avenue
New Hyde Park, NY 11040
> *For children with Cooley's anemia and their parents.*

Council of Adult Stutterers
c/o Speech and Hearing Clinic
Catholic University of America
Washington, DC 20017
> *For stutterers.*

Cystic Fibrosis Foundation
3379 Peachtree Road, N.E.
Atlanta, GA 30326
> *For persons with cystic fibrosis and their families.*

Daughters United
840 Guadelupe Parkway
San Jose, CA 95110
> *For young women.*

Delancey Street
3001 Pacific Avenue
San Francisco, CA 94115
> *For drug addicts.*

DES-Watch
360 Kent Street
Brookline, MA 02146
> *For women who took DES during pregnancy and their daughters.*

DES-Watch
P.O. Box 12
Wantaugh, NY 11793
> *For women who took DES during pregnancy and their daughters.*

Diet Workshop
28 Merrick Avenue
Merrick, NY 11566

Divorce Anonymous
P.O. Box 5313
Chicago, IL 60680
> *For divorced persons.*

Drop-Outs Anonymous
3876 E. Fedora Avenue
Fresno, CA 93726
> *For school and societal "drop-outs."*

Dysautonomia Association
608 Fifth Avenue
New York, NY 10020
> *For persons with genetic disorders of the autonomic nervous system.*

Easy Breathers, American Lung Association
1740 Broadway
New York, NY 10019
> *For persons with emphysema.*

El Centro de la Causa
831 West 17th Street
Chicago, IL 60608
> *An Hispanic mental health center.*

Emotional Health Anonymous
4328 Cumnor Road
Downers Grove, IL 60515
> *For persons with emotional problems.*

Emotions Anonymous
P.O. Box 4245
St. Paul, MN 55104
> *For persons with emotional problems.*

Emphysema Anonymous
P.O. Box 66
Fort Myers, FL 33902
> *For persons with emphysema.*

Epilepsy Foundation
1828 L Street, N.W.
Washington, DC 20036
> *For persons with epilepsy and their families.*

Families Anonymous
P.O. Box 344
Torrance, CA 90501
> *For families with problems.*

Fly Without Fear
42–60 Main Street
Flushing, NY 11355
> *For persons afraid of flying.*

The Fortune Society
29 East 22nd Street
New York, NY 10010
For ex-offenders and their families.

Gamblers Anonymous
P.O. Box 17173
Los Angeles, CA 90017
For gamblers.

Gamblers-Anon
P.O. Box 4549
Downey, CA 90241
For families of gamblers.

Gray Panthers
3700 Chestnut Street
Philadelphia, PA 19104
An activist senior citizens group (national headquarters).

Heart Clubs
7320 Greenville Avenue
Dallas, TX 75231
For persons who have had heart attacks and their families.

Hodgkins Disease and Lymphoma Organization
518 Wingate Drive
East Meadow, NY 11554
For persons with Hodgkins disease and their families.

Homecoming, Inc.
1132 West Pratt
Chicago, IL 60626
For former patients of mental institutions.

International Association of Laryngectomees
c/o American Cancer Society
777 Third Avenue
New York, NY 10017
For persons who have had larynx surgery and their families.

International Catholic Deaf Association
8419 Wesleyan Street
Vienna, VA 22180
 For deaf persons of the Catholic faith.

International Parents' Organization
c/o Alexander Graham Bell Association for the Deaf
1537 35th Street, N.W.
Washington, DC 20007
 For parents of deaf children.

Ladies Auxiliary
Military Order of the Purple Hearts
101 West Monument Street
Baltimore, MD 21201
 For wives of soldiers who have been wounded.

La Leche League
9616 Minneapolis Avenue
Franklin Park, IL 60131
 For nursing and new mothers.

The Learning Exchange
P.O. Box 920
Evanston, IL 60204
 For students who want to share teaching/learning.

Little People of America
Box 126
Owatonna, MN 55060
 For midgets and their families.

Make Today Count
Burlington, IA 52601
 For persons with cancer and their families.

Mended Hearts
2113 Ong Street
Amarillo, TX 79109
 For persons who have had heart attacks and their families.

Mensa
50 East 42nd Street
New York, NY 10017
>*For persons with high IQs.*

Mothers of Young Mongoloids
713 Ramsey Street
Alexandria, VA 22301
>*For mothers of young mongoloid children.*

Multiple Sclerosis
205 East 42nd Street
New York, NY 10017
>*For persons with multiple sclerosis and their families.*

Muscular Dystrophy Association
810 7th Avenue
New York, NY 10019
>*For persons with muscular dystrophy and their families.*

Myasthenia Gravis Foundation
230 Park Avenue
New York, NY 10017
>*For persons with myasthenia gravis and their families.*

Myopia International Research Foundation
415 Lexington Avenue,
Room 705
New York, NY 10017
>*For persons with myopia and their families.*

Nar-Anon Family Group
P.O. Box 2562
Palos Verdes Peninsula, CA 90274
>*For families of drug addicts.*

Narcotics Anonymous
P.O. Box 622
Sun Valley, CA 91352
>*For drug addicts,*

National Amputation Foundation
12–45 150th Street
Whitestone, NY 11357
  For amputees and their families.

National Association for Autistic Children
169 Tampa Avenue
Albany, NY 12208
  For autistic children and their families.

National Association for Down's Syndrome
628 Ashland
River Forest, IL 60305
  For children who have Down's Syndrome and their parents.

National Association for Gifted Children
8080 Springvalley Drive
Cincinnati, OH 45236
  For gifted children and their parents.

National Association for Help of
  Retarded Children
405 Lexington Avenue
New York, NY 10017
  For retarded children and their parents.

National Association for Retarded Children
2709 Avenue E, East
Arlington, TX 76011
  For retarded children and their parents.

National Association for the Deaf
814 Thayer Avenue
Silver Springs, MD 20910
  For deaf persons and their families.

National Association of the Physically
  Handicapped
6473 Grandville
Detroit, MI 48228
  For physically handicapped persons and their families

National Association of Patients on Hemodialysis
    and Transplantation
505 Northern Blvd.
Great Neck, NY 11021
    For persons with kidney illnesses and their families.

National Association of Recovered Alcoholics in
    the Professions (**NARAP**)
P.O. Box 95
Staten Island, NY 10305
    For alcoholics in medicine and other professions.

National Association to Aid Fat Americans
P.O. Box 745
Westbury, NY 11590
    For overweight persons.

National Congress of Organizations of the
    Physically Handicapped
7611 Oakland Avenue
Minneapolis, MN 55423
    A coalition of groups of handicapped persons.

National Congress of the Jewish Deaf
9102 Edmonston Court, No. 302
Greenbelt, MD 20770
    For deaf persons of the Jewish faith.

National Cystic Fibrosis Research Foundation
3379 Peachtree Road, N.E.
Atlanta, GA 30326
    For persons with cystic fibrosis and their families.

National Federation for the Blind
Suite 212, Dupont Circle
1346 Connecticut Avenue
Washington, DC 20036
    For blind persons and their families.

National Foundation for Ileitis and Colitis
295 Madison Avenue
New York, NY 10017
> *For persons with ileitis and colitis and their families.*

National Foundation for Sudden Infant Death
1501 Broadway
New York, NY 10036
> *For parents of children who have died of Sudden Infant Death Syndrome.*

National Fraternal Society of the Deaf
6701 West North Avenue
Oak Park, IL 60302
> *For deaf persons and their families.*

National Hemophilia Foundation
25 West 39 Street
New York, NY 10018
> *For hemophiliacs and their families.*

National Huntington Disease Association
Lakewood Center North Building
146 Detroit Avenue
Cleveland, OH 44107
> *For persons with Huntington's disease and their families.*

National Multiple Sclerosis
257 Park Avenue South
New York, NY 10010
> *For persons with multiple sclerosis and their families.*

National Organization for Non-Parents
515 Madison Avenue
New York, NY 10022
> *For married couples who choose not to have children.*

National Organization of Mothers of Twins Clubs
5402 Amberwood Lane
Rockville, MD 20853
> *For mothers of twins.*

National Paraplegia Foundation
400 East 34th Street
Room RR812
New York, NY 10016
    For paraplegiacs and their families.

National Rare Blood Club
c/o Associated Health Foundation
164 Fifth Avenue
New York, NY 10010
    For persons with rare blood diseases and their families.

National Society for Autistic Children
c/o Ruth Dyer
169 Tampa Avenue
Albany, NY 12208
    For autistic children and their parents.

National Tay-Sachs and Allied Diseases
        Association
122 East 42nd Street
New York, NY 10017
    For persons with Tay-Sachs disease and their families.

National Wheelchair Athletic Association
40–24 62nd Street
Woodside, NY 11377
    For physically handicapped persons.

Neurotics Anonymous International Liaison
1341 G Street, N.W.
Room 426
Washington, DC 20005
    For neurotics.

Orton Society
8415 Bellona Lane
Towson, MD 21204
    A clearinghouse for information about dyslexia.

Overeaters Anonymous
2365 Westwood Boulevard
Los Angeles, CA 90064
For overweight persons.

Paralyzed Veterans of America
7315 Wisconsin Avenue
Suite 301W
Washington, DC 20014
For paralyzed veterans and their families.

Parents Anonymous
2810 Artesia Blvd.
Redonda Beach, CA 90278
For parents of abused children.

Parents of Large Families
54 Miller Street
Fairfield, CT 06430
For parents of large families.

Parents Without Partners
7910 Woodmont Avenue
Washington, DC 20014
For single parents.

Phobia Self-Help Groups
White Plains Hospital
41 East Post Road
White Plains, NY 10601
For persons with phobias.

Prison Children Anonymous
129 Jackson Street
Hempstead, NY 11550
For children of prisoners.

Prison Families Anonymous
134 Jackson Street, LL4
Hempstead, NY 11550
For families of prisoners.

Psoriasis Research Association
107 Vista Del Grande
San Carlos, CA 94070
   For persons with psoriasis.

Reach to Recovery
American Cancer Society
19 West 56th Street
New York, NY 10019
   For women who have had mastectomies.

Recovery, Inc.
116 South Michigan Avenue
Chicago, IL 60603
   *For former patients of mental institutions and other persons
   with emotional problems.*

Retarded Infants Service
386 Park Avenue, South
New York, NY 10016
   For parents of retarded infants.

Schizophrenics Anonymous
1114 First Avenue
New York, NY 10021
   For schizophrenics.

Sisterhood of Black Single Mothers
P.O. Box 155
Brooklyn, NY 11203
   For Black single mothers.

Smoke Watchers
605 Third Avenue
New York, NY 10016
   For persons who wish to stop smoking.

Society for Rehabilitation of the Facially
      Disfigured
550 First Avenue
New York, NY 10016
   For facially disfigured persons and their families.

Spina Bifida Association
343 South Dearborn
Chicago, IL 60604
> *For persons with spina bifada and their families.*

Stroke Clubs
99 Carl Avenue
Franklin Square, NY 11010
> *For persons who have had strokes and their families.*

Sudden Infant Death Syndrome Foundation
310 South Michigan Avenue
Chicago, IL 60604
> *For parents of children who have died of Sudden Infant Death Syndrome.*

Synanon
P.O. Box 786
Marshall, CA 94940
> *For drug addicts and other persons who wish to follow the Synanon life-style.*

Take Off Pounds Sensibly
4575 South 5th Street
Milwaukee, WI 53207
> *For overweight persons.*

Tall Clubs, International
6515 Monte Avenue
Forty Wayne, IN 46815
> *For tall persons.*

United Cerebral Palsy Associations
66 East 34th Street
New York, NY 10016
> *For persons with cerebral palsy and their families.*

United Ostomy Association
1111 Wilshire Boulevard
Los Angeles, CA 90017
> *For persons who have had ostomy surgery.*

Weight Watchers
175 East Shore Road
Great Neck, NY 11023
        For overweight persons.

Widowed Inc.
1406 Spring Rock
Houston, TX 77055
        For widows.

Widow-To-Widow
c/o Laboratory of Community Psychiatry
Harvard Medical School
Cambridge, MA 02138
        For widows.

Appendix B

Similarities and Differences Between Conventional and Peer Self-Help Psychotherapy Groups (PSHPGs)

Nathan Hurvitz

䷱䷱䷱䷱䷱䷱䷱䷱䷱䷱䷱䷱䷱

A. Structural and Procedural Differences

CONVENTIONAL THERAPY	PSHPG
1. The therapist maintains authority and control.	1. Peers maintain authority and control.
2. The therapist sets the fee that is payment for his services; and he ensures that it will be paid.	2. Peers solicit free-will offerings that support their group and the fellowship of which it is a part.

Reprinted by permission from N. Hurvitz, "Similarities and Differences Between Conventional Psychotherapy and PSHPG's." In P. S. Roman and H. M. Trice (Eds.), *The Sociology of Psychotherapy.* New York: Aranson, 1974, pp. 110–120.

Authors' note: Although we are not in full agreement with Hurvitz (see Chapters Two and Five), his formulation is sufficiently rich, we believe, to warrant this full presentation.

3. The therapist keeps case records (which are withheld from the client).

3. No records are kept.

4. The therapist schedules private appointments (known only to the therapist, the client, and the client's family—and to those whom any one of them may choose to tell).

4. Peers attend meetings that are almost always open to the public and to which visitors and observers are invited.

5. Therapy sessions are scheduled according to a timetable and for a definite period of time.

5. Each group in the fellowship meets according to a timetable; however, any member can attend meetings of any group in the fellowship. Group meetings are indeterminate in length.

6. Therapy sessions do not follow a prescribed order.

6. Meetings tend to follow a regular, predetermined order of business.

7. The therapist may be seen outside the regularly scheduled appointments on an emergency basis.

7. Peers may call special or emergency meetings or one may call upon other peers as he needs them.

8. Therapy is conducted in hospitals, clinics, offices, and so on, specifically designed or established for this purpose and controlled by the therapist.

8. Meetings are conducted in halls, meeting rooms, homes, and so on, not designed or established for psychotherapy purposes but controlled by peers.

9. The therapist is required to have completed a program of professional education including clinical training under appropriate supervision; he is also required to be licensed, certified, and so on.

9. Peers are not required to have completed a program of professional education or to be licensed or certified; however, each fellowship or movement may have a training program that prepares its own members for greater responsibility within the fellowship.

10. The therapist determines therapy procedures and goals to help the client understand himself or to realize his fullest potential as an individual, as a precondition for solving his problems.

10. Peers determine therapy procedures and goals to help each other change specific behavior or solve a particular problem within the contest of their movement.

11. The therapist discourages his client from reading the scholarly or professional literature about his psychotherapeutic theories and methods.

11. Peers are encouraged to read the literature about their fellowship, which is displayed, distributed and sold at meetings, to learn its history, principles, effectiveness, and impact upon the community.

B. Reciprocity Between Therapist and Client and Between Peers

CONVENTIONAL THERAPY

PSHPG

1. A hierarchal or differential status exists between therapist and client; the therapist is the leader because of his socially defined and institutionalized role based upon his training, license, and so on.

1. A peer status exists in the fellowship's therapy activities; leaders are those who help others achieve their therapeutic goals.

2. The therapist does not fulfill role prescriptions that have been established by his clients.

2. Peers become therapists when they encourage and support others' efforts to change according to the principles of their fellowship.

3. The therapist (in contrast with the client) is successful, normal, healthy, mature, wise, and so on.

3. Peers acknowledge to each other that they are failures, abnormal, neurotic, immature, stupid, and so on.

4. The therapist does not have to experience the problem or behavior that defines the client: alcoholism, drug addiction, obesity, neuroticism, and so on.

4. All members of the fellowship have experienced the problem or behavior that defines them as peers: alcoholism, drug addiction, obesity, neuroticism, and so on.

5. The therapist does not reveal himself to the client.

5. Peers reveal themselves to each other.

6. The therapist, not having experienced and overcome the client's problem, is not a role model for his client.

6. Peers, having experienced and overcome the same problem, are role models for each other.

7. Because the therapist has not experienced and overcome the client's problem, the client may not identify with the therapist but may question his ability to understand him or help him change; the therapist does not become an instrumental significant other.

7. Because peers have experienced and overcome the same problem they do identify with each other; they know that each understands the other and can help the other change; peers become instrumental significant others.

8. The therapist's "difference" from the client prevents him from establishing "gut"-level interaction with the client, which is postulated as necessary for liberating insight and change.

8. The members' common problem encourages the establishment of "gut"-level interaction between them, which is postulated as necessary for liberating insight and change.

9. The therapist tends to regard the client as responsible for his lack of

9. Peers tend to regard themselves as responsible for each other's lack of

progress; the client's inability to achieve his asserted goal is his failure.

progress; a member's inability to achieve his goal as defined by the group's purpose is failure by the fellowship.

C. Moral Attitudes of the Therapist and Peers

CONVENTIONAL THERAPY

PSHPG

1. The therapist professes moral neutrality and is nonjudgmental, because he regards the client's deviant behavior as a medical problem that must be understood and not judged.

1. Peers profess a moral position and are judgmental, since behavior that is deviant, self-destructive, irresponsible, stupid, and so on should be changed even if it is a medical problem.

2. The therapist does not make the client feel guilty, ashamed, sinful, and so on.

2. Peers may make each other feel guilty, ashamed, sinful, and so on.

3. The therapist does not punish deviant, irresponsible, self-defeating behavior.

3. Peers may punish deviant, irresponsible, self-defeating behavior.

4. The therapist labels the client "sick," instead of expressing a moral judgment. The label may permit the client to deny responsibility for his behavior.

4. Peers' moral judgments about each other do not permit them to deny responsibility for their behavior.

5. The therapist considers the client "sick" and thereby justifies the client in his sick role. The client, playing the sick role, stays sick.

5. Peers may consider each other "sick," but they expect "well" behavior of each other. Peers, playing the well role, get well.

6. The therapist is areligious and tends to negate the importance of "spiritual" and "inspirational" activities.

6. Peers consider religious attitudes important and utilize "spiritual" and "inspirational" activities.

D. The Social and Psychological Systems of Therapists and Peers

CONVENTIONAL THERAPY

PSHPG

1. The psychodynamically oriented therapist has a diagnostic approach. He reviews the client's past to discover the causes of present problems.

1. Peers tend to be diagnostically oriented and review each other's past to discover the cause of present behavior and problems.

2. The therapist offers "insights" and "interpretations" on the basis of free associations, dreams, fantasies, slips of the tongue, and so on, that reveal

2. Peers offer insights and interpretations on the basis of unconscious processes and genetic and developmental material.

the client's unconscious processes or that are revealed through the discussion of genetic and developmental material.

3. The therapist seeks the "underlying causes" of the present problems, which he regards as symptoms, to preclude possible "symptom substitution" or greater problems such as depression, psychosis, or suicide.

3. Peers seek the underlying causes of the present problems, which they regard as symptoms; they are not concerned with symptom substitution or with greater problems if these causes are not discovered.

4. The therapist may foster psychological regression and evoke a transference neurosis as a therapeutic technique.

4. Peers do not foster psychological regression or evoke a transference neurosis.

5. The therapist regards any behavior that prevents the client from discovering the underlying cause of his problem as conscious or unconscious "resistance."

5. Peers regard any behavior that is not in accord with the member's asserted goal and therefore not in accord with the principles and goal of the fellowship as evidence of his unreadiness or unwillingness to accept the philosophy and discipline of the fellowship.

6. The therapist regards "symptomatic" or "acting out" behavior as evidence of the client's inability to control his instinctive impulses, his imperfect self-understanding, or his resistance to change because of the gratification gained from such behavior.

6. Peers regard deviant behavior as evidence of the member's irresponsibility, immaturity, lack of will power, or lack of desire to change.

7. The therapist keeps out of the therapy experience whatever may disturb the exploration of unconscious material.

7. Every aspect of the peer's functioning in the real world is subject to group review and evaluation.

8. The therapist develops and manipulates the "transference" relationship; he plays one role (or one role at a time), principally a parental or authority figure.

8. Peers interact with many others who play real life roles that are open to examination, and they experience various "transference" relationships directly.

9. The therapist regards the client's problems to be due to "unconscious conflicts," "death instincts," and so on, or to factors in his personal history that formed the client and over which he has no control; thus a client

9. Peers hold each other responsible for their behavior, regardless of its causes; they reject excuses that do not help the movement achieve its goals for them and may harm others. They urge responsibility for each

may believe that the therapist absolves him from responsibility for his problems.

other; require appropriate behavior in accord with the purpose of their movement. Their primary concern is with their own and others' behavior, and they support others' efforts and effective functioning by example, encouragement, "spotting," "endorsement," exhortation, ridicule, and so on, to achieve day-to-day goals.

10. The nondirective therapist responds to his client in the here-and-now and attempts to develop an effective therapeutic relationship based upon unconditional positive regard.

10. Peers respond to each other in the here-and-now and develop therapeutic relationships based upon honest confrontation in which they express negative as well as positive views.

11. The therapist attempts to enhance the client's self-attitudes to achieve self-actualization and the realization of his human potential.

11. Peers attempt to help each other solve specific problems or deviant behavior; and by the successful accomplishment of these goals they help each other achieve self-actualization and the realization of each member's human potential.

12. The psychodynamic and nondirective therapists tend to be passive in their relationship with the client. Each assumes that through their procedures and techniques they will either help the client understand his intrapsychic processes or help him gain enhanced self-attitudes; in this way each will enable the client to solve his specific problems.

12. Peers are active in their relationship with each other. They focus on the presenting problem, emphasize activity, and assume that by following the principles and practices of their movement they will help the member solve his specific problems and thereby cause intrapsychic changes and enhanced self-attitudes.

13. Neither therapist ridicules the client or expresses his hostile feelings toward the client.

13. Peers may ridicule and attack each other with great hostility, and they may provoke aggressive and hostile feelings. However, peers regard such attacks and provocations as others' expressions of concern and care.

14. Both therapists give, and the client receives, support.

14. Peers give as well as receive support.

15. Both therapists assume that gains in the psychotherapy setting will be

15. Peers assume that the fellowship experience will be transferred into

25. Both therapists' scheduled appointments are part of a series in which the client is removed from his real-life experience.

25. Each meeting of the fellowship involves the member in activities and relationships that become part of his real-life experiences.

26. Both therapists may be the only supporters of the client's effort to change.

26. Peers are members of a community, each member of which supports the others' efforts to change.

27. Each client is one among others of the therapists' clients.

27. Each member is a peer among others who participate in a fellowship or movement.

28. The therapy experience encourages self-involvement.

28. The fellowship experience encourages involvement with others.

29. The client's preferred or desired behavior occurs randomly, and both therapists reinforce it haphazardly.

29. Peers give each other periodic support in accordance with a meeting schedule and continuing support by their availability to each other. Appropriate behavior is defined and required by membership in the fellowship; such behavior is encouraged but not planfully reinforced.

30. Both therapists learn and keep their clients' secrets private.

30. Peers disclose their secrets in public.

31. Both therapists, as "significant others," represent "generalized others" and symbolically accept the clients for the community, despite their harmful behavior toward others.

31. Peers' knowledge of each other's secrets is "punishment" for behavior that may be associated with present problems and serves to expiate their guilt feelings. Thus peers do not represent significant others, they are significant others; each one's acceptance of the other is not symbolic but real.

32. Neither therapist encourages the client to make restitution to those whom he has harmed in some way.

32. Peers encourage each other to make restitution to those whom they may have harmed in some way.

33. Both therapists determine which clients they will accept and tend to select those who are younger, intelligent, educated, verbal, attractive, and able to pay for private psychotherapy and to function despite their deviance or problem.

33. Peers do not select each other; anyone who has the problem that defines their fellowship is eligible for membership, and they have a hopeful attitude about helping anyone who joins their movement. At the same time they will not jeopardize their movement because of a peer's deviant behavior, which may threaten

34. The client has no impact upon the community and no status in the client role.

34. Peers encourage involvement with others by participation in a social movement. As members of this social movement, which has novelty and positive aspects, peers make an impact upon the community, have status as members of their fellowship, and thereby gain self-esteem.

the well-being of others or of their movement. They may expel such a member.

35. The client does not have an opportunity for mobility to various positions in the therapy setting.

35. Peers have an opportunity for mobility to various positions within the fellowship.

36. The client never achieves the status or performs the role of the therapists.

36. All peers are considered therapists.

37. Neither therapist organizes community groups to support the therapeutic ideology with which they are identified; however, clients may do so.

37. Peers organize community groups to support their movement and publicize it in every way they can.

38. The client continues to live in a setting that constrains him in his established behavior, and the therapists return the clients with whom they have been successful, as well as those with whom they have not been successful, to this setting at the conclusion of therapy.

38. Peers who have had an unsuccessful experience in the fellowship drop away (and are not known to new members), while those who have solved their problems maintain a place in the social system of their movement and are responsible for aiding and training others to whom they serve as role models.

E. Group Therapy with Therapists and Peers

CONVENTIONAL THERAPY

1. Therapy is primarily individual, and group therapy is one modality used by the therapist.

PSHPG

1. All therapy occurs in groups; individuals may form shifting therapeutic dyads within the structure of the fellowship.

2. The therapist always controls the group because of his status gained prior to and outside the group.

2. Group leadership develops and is assumed by different members as they help others achieve the movement's purpose and thereby solve their problems.

3. The therapist's consideration is "What is in the best interests of each individual member?"

4. The therapist regards the client's inability to fit into the group as an aspect of his problems, which he does not complicate by denying him admission or rejecting him from the group.

5. Clients tend to be similar in many ways: race, education, economic level, and so on.

6. Clients with different problems and histories, who are not role models for each other, may participate in the same group.

7. The client's achievements gained prior to and outside the group—his profession, wealth, how well known he is—may affect his status in the group.

8. Clients achieve status in the group by emulating the therapist's activity and assuming an "associate therapist" role in relation to him.

9. The client's observed behavior in group interaction is assumed to be a sample of his "real," characteristic behavior.

10. Clients may withhold information about themselves and still maintain a place in the group; clients therefore have limited knowledge about each other.

11. Clients may interact on the basis of group norms during the group

3. The peers' consideration is "What is in the best interest of the movement?" In this way, each member serves himself and the others best.

4. Peers regard another's inability to fit into their movement not only as an aspect of his problem but also as a threat to the movement. They may deny admission or reject from the fellowship anyone who may damage or destroy it.

5. Peers tend to be different in many ways, other than their common problem: race, age, education, economic level, and so on.

6. Peers with similar problems and histories, who are role models for each other, are members of the fellowship.

7. A member's achievements gained prior to and outside the movement—his profession, wealth, how well known he is—affect his status in the group. He may be treated more severely if he attempts to use his achievements to impress others.

8. Peers achieve status in the movement by indicating the contrast between their former and present behavior, by helping others, by serving as "sponsors," and by undertaking greater responsibility in their movement.

9. Members continually interact so all know each other's "real," characteristic behavior.

10. Peers must and do share all information about themselves and have complete knowledge about each other.

11. Members' interaction continues before and after meetings so members

meeting; however, they may behave on the basis of deviant norms outside the group meeting.

observe each other's behavior and exert pressure to make it conform with fellowship norms.

12. Since groups meet once or twice a week, the group offers limited opportunities for clients to experience self-examination, self-assessment, behavior change, and so on, and to attempt to change real-life behavior and attitudes.

12. Peer interaction is a continuously available opportunity for self-examination, self-assessment, peer assessment, and behavior change. The fellowship offers opportunities for peers to have real-life meaning for each other and to change real-life behavior and attitudes.

13. Group members do not have real-life meaning for each other; they are self-concerned individuals who are incidentally concerned with others as they attempt to solve their own problems and change their behavior. They are not interdependent in their efforts to change problem behavior.

13. Peers have real-life meaning for each other and assist each other to change real-life behavior and attitudes. Peers are aware of their interdependence, and they are concerned about their own and the others' efforts to solve their problems, to change their behavior, proving the validity of the movement to which they have committed themselves.

14. Clients resist imposing on other group members outside of scheduled group meetings. At the same time, the therapist discourages clients' contacts outside the group because of possible damaging contact, mutual exploitation, and so on.

14. Peers are always and immediately available to each other and being called upon by another for help is a mark of esteem that is highly regarded and reinforces the value of the movement.

F. Therapist's Professional Identification and Peers' Fellowship Identification

CONVENTIONAL THERAPY

1. The therapist's professional status ascribes to him the ultimate source of wisdom in the therapist-client interaction.

PSHPG

1. Different members are regarded as a source of wisdom as they function characteristically in various situations to help their peers achieve their goals. Where professional therapists participate in the fellowship, they play an auxiliary role and are dominated by the group members.

2. The therapist's professional status and his identification with a specific psychotherapeutic ideology and technique may restrict experimentation and inhibit creativity.

2. The peers' identification is with their movement, they are not concerned about functioning as therapists, so they may introduce innovations in psychotherapy.

3. The therapist's economic dependence upon his clients may make him vulnerable to their manipulation.

3. Peer relationships have no economic aspect, and peers are not vulnerable to manipulation on this basis.

4. The client may participate in psychotherapy activities that he questions, because the therapist's authority is imposed upon him, because of his dependent status, or because the therapist's function is institutionalized and societally accepted.

4. Members participate in the fellowship voluntarily and accept the helping activities of their peers only as long as they want to.

5. The therapist represents and accepts the community and its authority, values, and so on.

5. The fellowship represents and accepts the community and its authority, values, and so on, which the peers accept.

6. The client may not have the means for mobility and success in the therapist's world because of his deviant behavior or psychological problems.

6. Peers are members of a movement that encourages mobility within the fellowship itself; peers become successful according to the ways and values of their movement.

7. The client becomes dependent upon the therapist, which is just like being dependent upon his addiction (if this is his problem), or it becomes a substitute problem.

7. A member may become dependent upon the movement, which is just like being dependent upon his addiction (if this is his problem), or it becomes a substitute problem.

8. The client has faith in the therapist on the basis of his status and reputation in the professional community, his own knowledge of the therapist's helpfulness, and the status of the referring person.

8. Peers have faith in each other because of the success of their movement in aiding others with problems like their own.

9. The client may not regard the therapist as someone with power greater than his own, which could create an expectation of help and thereby become a source of help to the client.

9. Peers encourage each other to acknowledge that there is a power greater than themselves that they can call upon for help and that is a source of help to them.

10. Community attitudes to conventional therapy range from unfriendly to active support; in general, they are tolerant and accepting.

10. Community attitudes to the fellowship range from hostility to active support; in general, they are skeptical and resistant.

References

ABRAHAMS, R. B. "Mutual Aid for the Widowed." *Social Work*, 1972, *17*, 54–61.

ABRAHAMS, R. B. "Mutual Helping: Styles of Caregiving in a Mutual Aid Program—The Widowed Service Line." In G. Caplan and M. Killilea (Eds.), *Support Systems and Mutual Help: Multidisciplinary Explorations*. New York: Grune & Stratton, 1976.

Advisory Committee to the Renal Transplant Registry. "Twelfth Report of the Human Renal Transplant Registry." *Journal of the American Medical Association*, 1975, *223*, 787–791.

ALLEN, V. L. (Ed.) *Children as Teachers*. New York: Academic, 1976.

ALLON, N. "Group Dieting Rituals." *Society*, 1973, *10*, 36–42.

ALMOND, R. *The Healing Community: Dynamics of the Therapeutic Milieu*. New York: Aronson, 1974.

ANTZE, P. "The Role of Ideologies in Peer Psychotherapy Organizations: Some Theoretical Considerations and Three Case Studies." *Journal of Applied Behavioral Science*, 1976, *12*, 323–346.

BABAGIAN, J. "Gavel Raps." *Notebook*, 1976–77, *17*, 1–5.

BARISH, H. "Self-Help Groups." *Encyclopedia of Social Work*, 1971, 2, 1164.

BASSIN, A. "Daytop Village." *Psychology Today*, 1968, *2*, 48–52.

BOOZ, and ALLEN. Public Administration Services, Inc. *Cost-Benefit Study of the Foster Grandparents Program*. Washington, D.C.: ACTION, 1975.

BOOZ, ALLEN, and HAMILTON. *Senior Companions Program Study, Phases I and II*. Washington, D.C.: ACTION, 1975.

BORMAN, L. D. (Ed.) *Explorations in Self-Help and Mutual Aid*. Proceedings of the Self-Help Workshop held June 9–12, 1974, in Chicago, under the auspices of the W. Clement and Jessie W. Stone Foundation. Evanston, Ill.: Northwestern University, Center for Urban Affairs, 1975.

Boston Women's Health Collective. *Our Bodies, Ourselves: A Book by and for Women*. New York: Simon & Schuster, 1972.

BOWLES, E. "Older Persons as Providers of Services: Three Federal Programs." *Social Policy*, 1976, *7*, 81–88.

BRENNER, M. H. "Estimating the Social Costs of National Economic Policy: Implications for Mental and Physical Health and Criminal Aggression." Unpublished paper prepared for the Congressional Joint Economic Committee, U.S. Congress, Washington, D.C. 20515, October 26, 1976.

Brief Guide to Alcoholics Anonymous, A. New York: Alcoholics Anonymous World Services, 1975.

BROWN, C. C. "It Changed My Life." *Psychology Today*, 1976, *10*, 47–54.

BROWN, W. F. "Effectiveness of Paraprofessionals: The Evidence." *The Personnel and Guidance Journal*, 1974, *53*, 257–263.

BROZAN, N. "Repercussions of a Drug." *New York Times*, June 17, 1976, p. 41.

CAPLAN, G. *Support Systems and Community Mental Health: Lectures on Concept Development*. New York: Behavioral Publications, 1974.

CAPLAN, G., and KILLILEA, M. (Eds.). *Support Systems and Mutual Help: Multidisciplinary Explorations*. New York: Grune & Stratton, 1976.

CARTER, T. "The Career Opportunities Program: A Summing Up." *COP Bulletin*, 1976, *3*, 1–37.

CHERKAS, M. S. "Synanon Foundation—A Radical Approach to the

Problem of Addiction." *American Journal of Psychiatry,* 1965, *121,* 1065–1068.

CLINARD, M. *Sociology of Deviant Behavior.* New York: Holt, Rinehart and Winston, 1963.

CLOWARD, R. "Studies in Tutoring." *The Journal of Experimental Education,* 1967, *36,* 14–25.

COLLIER, P. "The House of Synanon." *Ramparts,* 1967, *6,* 93.

CREIGHTON, L. B. *Pretenders to the Throne.* Lexington, Mass.: Lexington Books, 1976.

CRESSEY, D. R. "Social Psychological Foundations for Using Criminals in the Rehabilitation of Criminals." *Journal of Research on Crime and Delinquency,* 1965, *2,* 49–59.

DAWSON, R. W. K. "Personality and Peer Counsellors: An Australian Study." *The Personnel and Guidance Journal,* 1973, *52,* 46–48.

DEAN, S. R. "Self-Help Groups Psychotherapy: Mental Patients Rediscover Will Power." *International Journal of Social Psychiatry,* 1971, *17,* 72–78.

DELWORTH, U. (Ed.). "Special Issue: Paras, Peers, and Pros." *The Personnel and Guidance Journal,* 1974, *53,* 249–340.

DEWAR, T. "Professionalized Clients as Self-Helpers." In *Self-Help and Health: A Report.* New York: City University of New York, Queens College, New Human Service Institute, 1976.

Directory of Mutual Help Organizations in Massachusetts, A. Boston: Blue Cross and Blue Shield of Massachusetts, 1974.

DOLLAR, B. "If You Need a Shoulder, I Have Two." Unpublished manuscript. New York: National Commission on Resources for Youth, 1976.

DRISCOLL, C. B., and LUBIN, A. H. "Conferences with Parents of Children with Cystic Fibrosis." *Social Casework,* 1972, *53,* 140–146.

DUMONT, M. P. "Self-Help Treatment Programs." *American Journal of Psychiatry,* 1974, *131,* 631–635.

DURMAN, E. C. "The Role of Self-Help in Service Provision." *Journal of Applied Behavioral Science,* 1976, *12,* 433–443.

EBERLY, D. "Universal Youth Service." *Social Policy,* 1977, *7,* 43–46.

E. F. SHELLEY AND CO. *Study of Retired Senior Volunteer Programs.* Washington, D.C.: ACTION, 1973.

EGELSON, J., and EGELSON, J. F. *Parents Without Partners.* New York: Dutton, 1961.

EHRENREICH, B. "Letter to the Editor." *Social Policy,* 1974, *4,* 56.

ENRIGHT, J. B. "Synanon: A Challenge to Middle-Class Views of

Mental Health." In D. Adelson and B. L. Kales (Eds.), *Community Psychology and Mental Health: Perspectives and Challenges*. Scranton, Pa.: Chandler, 1970.

ERIKSON, E. H. *Identity and the Life Crisis*. New York: International Universities Press, 1959.

"Fact Sheet: What Is TOPS?" Milwaukee: TOPS Club, 1975.

FESTINGER, L. "A Theory of Social Comparison Processes." *Human Relations*, 1954, *7*, 117–140.

FLECKENSTEIN, L. "Oral Contraceptives Patient Information: A Questionnaire Study of Attitudes, Knowledge, and Preferred Information Sources." *Journal of the American Medical Association*, 1976, *225*, 17–28.

FOA, V. C., and FOA, E. B. "Resource Exchange: Toward a Structured Theory of Interpersonal Communication." In A. W. Siegman and B. Pope, (Eds.), *Studies in Dyadic Communication*. Elmsford, N.Y.: Pergamon, 1971.

FREDERICKSON, D. T. "The Community's Response to Substance Misuse: New York City Smoking Withdrawal Clinic." *International Journal of Addictions*, 1968, *3*, 81–89.

FRY, J. "Role of the Patient in Primary Health Care: The Viewpoint of the Medical Practitioner." Paper presented to the Symposium on the Role of the Individual in Primary Health Care, Institute of Social Medicine, University of Copenhagen, Denmark, August 11–15, 1975.

FUCHS, V. *The Service Economy*. New York: Columbia University Press, 1968.

FUCHS, V. *Who Shall Live?* New York: Basic Books, 1974.

GARTNER, A. *Paraprofessionals and Their Performance*. New York: Praeger, 1971.

GARTNER, A. *The Preparation of Human Services Professionals*. New York: Human Sciences Press, 1976.

GARTNER, A., JACKSON, V. C., and RIESSMAN, F. *Paraprofessionals in Education Today*. New York: Human Sciences Press, 1977.

GARTNER, A., KOHLER, M. C., and RIESSMAN, F. *Children Teach Children: Learning by Teaching*. New York: Harper & Row, 1971.

GARTNER, A., and RIESSMAN, F. *The Service Society and the Consumer Vanguard*. New York: Harper & Row, 1974.

GERSON, E. M., and STRAUSS, A. L. "Time for Living: Problems in Chronic Illness Care." *Social Policy*, 1975, *6*, 12–18.

GLASER, F. "Gaudenzia, Incorporated: Historical and Theoretical Background of a Self-Help Addiction Treatment Program." *International Journal of Addictions*, 1971, *6*, 615–626.

GLASSCOTE, R. M. *The Alternative Services: Their Role in Mental Health, a Field Study of Free Clinics, Runaway Houses, Counseling Centers, and the Like*. Washington, D.C.: Joint Information Center, 1975.

GOFFMAN, E. *Stigma: Notes on the Management of Spoiled Identities*. Englewood Cliffs, N.J.: Prentice-Hall, 1963.

GORDON, J. S. "Hotline: Self-Help Among the Helpers." *Social Policy*, 1976, *7*, 48–52.

GOULD, E. P. "Special Report: The Single-Parent Family Benefits in Parents Without Partners, Inc." *Journal of Marriage and the Family*, 1968, *30*, 666–671.

GOULDNER, A. W. "The Norm of Reciprocity: A Preliminary Statement." *The American Sociological Review*, 1960, *25*, 161–179.

GREEN, L. W., WERLIN, S. H., and SCHAUFFLER, H. M. "Research and Demonstration Issues in Self-Care: Measuring the Decline of Mediocentrism." Paper prepared for the Conference on Self-Care Programs, National Center for Health Services Research, Rockville, Maryland, March 25–26, 1976.

GROSZ, H. J. *Recovery, Inc., Survey*. Chicago: Recovery, Inc., 1972.

GUERNEY, B. "Filial Therapy: Description and Rationale." *Journal of Consulting Psychology*, 1964, *28*, 304–310.

GUSSOW, Z., and TRACY, G. S. "Interim Status Report: Voluntary Self-Help Health Organizations, a Study in Human Support Systems." Unpublished manuscript, Louisiana State University, Baton Rouge, LA, 1973.

GUSSOW, Z., and TRACY, G. S. "The Role of Self-Help Clubs in Adaptation to Chronic Illness and Disability." Unpublished manuscript, undated.

HAMBERG, B. A., and VARENHORST, B. B. "Peer Counseling in the Secondary School." *American Journal of Orthopsychiatry*, 1972, *42*, 566–581.

HAMPDEN-TURNER, C. *Sane Asylum*. San Francisco: San Francisco Book Company, 1976.

"Helpers." *Newsday*, October 16, 1976, pp. 2A–11A.

HESS, B. B. (Ed.) *Growing Old in America*. New Brunswick, N.J.: Transaction Books, 1976a.

HESS, B. B. "Support Systems and Self-Help." *Social Policy*, 1976b, *7*, 55–62.

HOCHSCHILD, A. R. "Communal Life-Styles for the Old." *Society*, 1973, *10*, 50–58.

"The Honeymoon Is Almost Over." *Frontiers*, 1975, pp. 1–2.

HORNSTEIN, F., DOWNER, C., and FARBER, S. "Gynecological Self-Help." In *Self-Help and Health: A Report*. New York: Queens College, New Human Services Institute, 1976.

HOWELL, M. C. *Helping Ourselves: Families and the Human Network*. Boston: Beacon, 1975a.

HOWELL, M. C. "A Women's Health School." *Social Policy*, 1975b, *6*, 50–53.

HURVITZ, N. "Peer Self-Help Psychotherapy Groups: Psychotherapy Without Psychotherapists." In R. B. Trice (Ed.), *The Sociology of Psychotherapy*. New York: Aronson, 1974.

HURVITZ, N. "The Origins of the Peer Self-Help Psychotherapy Group Movement." *Journal of Applied Behavioral Sciences*, 1976, *12*, 283–294.

I Am a Parents Anonymous Parent. Redondo Beach, Calif.: Parents Anonymous, Inc., 1974.

ILLICH, I. "Age of Professional Dominance." Unpublished manuscript, CIDOC, Cuernavaca, Mexico, 1976.

Intergroup Association of Alcoholics Anonymous of Greater New York. *AA Meetings in the Greater New York Area*. New York: Alcoholics Anonymous World Services, October 9, 1976.

The International Association of Laryngectomees Directory, 1976. New York: International Association of Laryngectomees, 1976.

JENCKS, S. F. "Problems in Participatory Health Care." In *Self-Help and Health: A Report*. New York: Queens College, New Human Services Institute, 1976.

JOHNSON, J. E., and PEEBLES, O. W. "Use of a Self-Help Community Model in the Treatment of Adolescent Behavior Disorders." *Adolescence*, 1973, *29*, 67–84.

JOHNSON, S. K. *Idle Haven: Community Building Among the Working-Class Retired*. Berkeley: University of California Press, 1971.

JOHNSTON, D. F. "The Future of Work: Three Possible Alternatives." *Monthly Labor Review*, 1972, *95*, 23–27.

KATZ, A. H. "Application of Self-Help Concepts in Current Social Welfare." *Social Work*, 1965, *10*, 68–74.

KATZ, A. H. "Marginal Man and the States of the Handicapped in Our Society." Paper presented at the National Conference on Life Enrichment Needs of Persons with Multiple Handicaps Who Are Socially and Culturally Deprived, Alexandria, Virginia, March 1970a.

KATZ, A. H. "Self-Help Organizations and Volunteer Participation in Social Welfare." *Social Work,* 1970b, *15,* 51–60.

KATZ, A. H. "Self-Help Groups." *Social Work,* 1972, *17,* 120–121.

KATZ, A. H. "Self-Help and the Handicapped." *New Society,* April 10, 1975a, pp. 13–15.

KATZ, A. H. "Some Thoughts on Self-Help Groups and the Professional Community." Paper presented at the National Conference on Social Welfare, San Francisco, May 1975b.

KATZ, A. H., and BENDER, E. I. (Eds.). *The Strength in Us: Self-Help Groups in the Modern World.* New York: New Viewpoints, 1976.

KELLY, H. J. "The Effect of the Helping Experience upon the Self-Concept of the Helper." Unpublished doctoral dissertation, University of Pittsburgh, 1973.

KILLILEA, M. "Mutual Help Organizations: Interpretations in the Literature." In G. Caplan and M. Killilea (Eds.), *Support Systems and Mutual Help: Multidisciplinary Explorations.* New York: Grune & Stratton, 1976.

KING, B. T., and JANIS, I. L. "Comparison of the Effectiveness of Improvised Versus Role Playing Producing Opinion Changes." *Human Relations,* 1956, *1,* 177–186.

KIRSCHBAUM, H. R., HARVESTON, D. S., and KATZ, A. H. "Independent Living for the Disabled." *Social Policy,* 1976, *7,* 59–62.

KLEEMAN, M. J., and DE PREE, J. L. "Self-Help Groups and Their Effectiveness as Agents for Chronic Illness Care: The Case of Kidney Transplant Patients." In *Self-Help and Health: A Report.* New York: City University of New York, Queens College, New Human Services Institute, 1976.

KLEIMAN, M. A., MANTEL, J. E., and ALEXANDER, E. S. "Collaboration and Its Discontents: The Perils of Partnership." *Journal of Applied Behavioral Science,* 1976, *12,* 403–409.

KNAPP, V. S., and HANSEN, H. "Helping Parents of Children with Leukemia." *Social Work,* 1973, *18,* 70–75.

LANDY, D., and SINGER, S. E. "The Social Organization and Culture of a Club of Former Mental Patients." *Human Relations,* 1961, *14,* 31–41.

Laryngectomees at Work. New York: International Association of Laryngectomees, 1975.

Laryngectomized Speakers' Source Book. New York: International Association of Laryngectomees, 1975.

LEE, D. T. "Recovery, Inc.: A Well-Role Model." *Mental Hygiene,* 1971, *55,* 194–198.

LEE, D. T. "Therapeutic Type: Recovery, Inc." In A. H. Katz and E. Bender (Eds.), *The Strength in Us: Self-Help Groups in the Modern World.* New York: New Viewpoints, 1976.

LENNENBERG, E., and ROWBOTHAM, J. L. *The Iliostomy Patient.* Springfield, Ill.: Thomas, 1970.

LEVIN, L. "The Layperson as the Primary Care Practitioner." *Public Health Reports,* 1976a, *91,* 206–210.

LEVIN, L. "Self-Care: An International Perspective." *Social Policy,* 1976b, *7,* 70–76.

LEVIN, L., KATZ, A. H., and HOLST, E. *Self-Care: Lay Initiatives in Health.* New York: Prodist, 1976.

LEVINE, M., and LEVINE, A. *A Social History of the Helping Services: Clinic, Court, School, and Community.* New York: Appleton-Century-Crofts, 1970.

LEVY, L. H. "Self-Help Groups: Types and Psychological Processes." *Journal of Applied Behavioral Science,* 1976, *12,* 310–313.

LEWIS, D. A. "Insuring Women's Health." *Social Policy,* 1976, *7,* 19–25.

LEWIS, J. A., and LEWIS, M. A. *Community Counseling: A Human Services Approach.* New York: Wiley, 1976.

LEWIS, M. A. "Child-Initiated Care." *American Journal of Nursing,* 1974, *74,* 652–655.

LIEBER, L. "Parents Anonymous." *Child Abuse and Neglect Reports,* 1976, *3,* 1–2.

LIEBERMAN, M. A., and BOND, G. R. "The Problem of Being a Woman: A Survey of 1700 Women in Consciousness-Raising Groups." *Journal of Applied Behavioral Science,* 1976, *12,* 363–380.

LIEBERMAN, M. A., and BORMAN, L. D. "Self-Help and Social Research." *Journal of Applied Behavioral Science,* 1976a, *12,* 455–463.

LIEBERMAN, M. A., and BORMAN, L. D. (Eds.). "Special Issue: Self-Help Groups." *Journal of Applied Behavioral Science,* 1976b, *12,* 261–463.

Like Mastectomy, Ostomy Surgery Needs More Public Exposure. (Press Release.) Los Angeles: United Ostomy Association, n.d.

LIPPITT, P., EISEMAN, J., and LIPPITT, R. *Cross-Age Helping Programs.* Ann Arbor: University of Michigan, 1969.

LISS, J. *Free to Feel: Finding Your Way Through the New Therapies.* New York: Praeger, 1974.

LOW, A. A. *Mental Health Through Will Training.* Boston: Christopher, 1950.

LURIE, A., and RON, H. "Self-Help in an Aftercare Socialization Program." *Mental Hygiene,* 1971, *55,* 467–472.

References 197

LYNCH, W., JR. Testimony Presented Before the Sub-Committee on Health, Committee on Interstate and Foreign Commerce, U.S. House of Representatives, Washington, D.C. 20515, November 10, 1975.

MARIESKIND, H. I. "Helping Oneself to Health." *Social Policy,* 1976, 7, 63–66.

MARIESKIND, H. I., and EHRENREICH, B. "Toward Socialist Medicine: The Women's Health Movement." *Social Policy,* 1975, 6, 34–42.

MILIO, N. "Self-Care in Urban Settings." Paper presented at the American Public Health Association Annual Meetings, Miami, Florida, October 19, 1976.

MORRIS, J. "Alcoholics Anonymous." In E. D. Whitney (Ed.), *World Dialogue on Alcohol and Drug Dependence.* Boston: Beacon Press, 1970.

MOWRER, O. H. *Conflict, Contract, Conscience, and Confession.* Urbana: University of Illinois Press, 1971a.

MOWRER, O. H. *Integrity Groups Today.* Urbana: University of Illinois Press, 1971b.

MOWRER, O. H. "Peer Groups and Medication, the 'Best' Therapy for Professionals and Laymen Alike." *Psychotherapy: Theory, Research, and Practice,* 1971c, 8, 44–54.

MOWRER, O. H. *The New Group Therapy.* Princeton, N.J.: D. Van Nostrand, 1974.

MOWRER, O. H., and VATTANO, A. J. *Integrity Groups: The Loss and Recovery of Community.* Urbana, Ill.: Integrity Groups, 1974.

MOWRER, O. H., and VATTANO, A. J. "Integrity Groups: A Context for Growth in Honesty, Responsibility, and Involvement." *Journal of Applied Behavioral Science,* 1976, 12, 419–431.

MURPHY, A., PEUSCHEL, S. M., and SCHNEIDER, J. "Group Work with Parents of Children with Down's Syndrome." *Social Casework,* 1973, 54, 114–119.

Narcotics Anonymous. Sun Valley, Calif.: Narcotics Anonymous World Services Organization, 1976.

Neurotics Anonymous: An Introduction. Washington, D.C.: Neurotics Anonymous International Liaison, 1966.

NEWMARK, G. *This School Belongs to You and Me: Every Learner a Teacher, Every Teacher a Learner.* New York: Hart, 1976.

NEWMARK, J., and NEWMARK, S. "Older Persons in a Planned Community: Synanon." *Social Policy,* 1976, 7, 93–99.

"News from TOPS." Milwaukee TOPS Clubs, Inc., 4575 South Fifth, Milwaukee, Wisc. 53207, 1975.

OFSHE, R. "Social Structure and Social Control in Synanon." *Journal of Voluntary Action Research,* 1974, *3,* 67–76.

PALMER, M. B. "Social Rehabilitation for Mental Patients." *Mental Hygiene,* 1968, *52,* 24–28.

Parents Anonymous: Chapter Development Manual. Redondo Beach, Calif.: Parents Anonymous, Inc., 1974.

PARK, C. C. *You Are Not Alone.* Boston: Little, Brown, 1976.

PARSONS, S., and TAGLIARENI, E. M. "Cancer Patients Help Each Other." *American Journal of Nursing,* 1974, *74,* 650–651.

PARSONS, T. *The Social System.* New York: Free Press, 1951.

PEARL, A. "Youth in Lower Class Settings." Paper presented at the Fifth Symposium on Social Psychology, University of Oklahoma, Norman, Oklahoma, 1964.

PEARL, A., and RIESSMAN, F. *New Careers for the Poor.* New York: Free Press, 1965.

PEARLMAN, M. "If You Need a Shoulder, I Have Two." Unpublished manuscript, National Commission on Resources for Youth, 36 West 44th St., New York, NY 10036, 1976.

PELLMAN, D. R. "Learning to Live with Dying." *New York Times Magazine,* December 5, 1976, pp. 44, 71, 75, 78, 80, 82, 85.

PERLMAN, J. E. "Grassrooting the System." *Social Policy,* 1976, *7,* 4–20.

PETRILLO, R. "The Rap Room." *Social Policy,* 1976, *7,* 54–58.

PHILLIPS, J. *Alcoholics Anonymous: An Annotated Bibliography, 1935–1972.* Cincinnati, Ohio: Central Ohio Publishing, 1973.

RABINOWITZ, H. S., and ZIMMERLIN, W. H. "Teaching-Learning Mechanisms in Consumer Health Education." *Public Health Reports,* 1976, *91,* 211–217.

RANNEY, J. "Help for the Laryngectomee." *Physician's Management,* 1969, 75–S.

RANNEY, J. "Rehabilitation Through Employment." *The Laryngoscope,* 1975, *85,* 674–676.

Recovery: What It Is and How It Developed. Chicago: Recovery, Inc., 1973.

RICKER, G. A. "The Little People of America." *Personnel and Guidance Journal,* 1970, *48,* 663–664.

RIESSMAN, F. "The 'Helper-Therapy' Principle." *Social Work,* 1965, *10,* 27–32.

RIESSMAN, F. "The Self-Help Movement Has Arrived." *Social Policy,* 1976, *6,* 63–64.

RITCHIE, O. W. "A Socio-Historical Analysis of Alcoholics Anonymous." *Quarterly Journal of Studies on Alcohol,* 1948, *9,* 119–156.

ROBERTSON, N. "For Cancer Patients and Their Families, Dishonesty May Also Be an Enemy." *New York Times*, November 24, 1976, p. 28.

SAGARIN, E. *Odd Man In*. New York: Quadrangle Books, 1969.

SAINER, J. "The Community Cares: Elderly Volunteers." *Social Policy*, 1976, *7*, 73–75.

SALES, G. *John Maher of Delancey Street*. New York: Norton, 1976.

SANDERS, D. H. "Patients-75; Professional-0: The Lodge Program in Community Rehabilitation." In A. H. Katz and E. Bender (Eds.), *The Strength in Us: Self-Help in the Modern World*. New York: New Viewpoints, 1976.

SCHLOPER, E., and LOFTIN, J. "Thinking Disorders in Parents of Young Psychotic Children." *Journal of Abnormal Psychology*, 1969, *74*, 281–287.

SCHLOPER, E., and REICHLER, R. J. "Parents as Co-Therapists in the Treatment of Psychotic Children." *Journal of Autism and Childhood Schizophrenia*, 1971, *1*, 87–102.

SCHOFIELD, W. *Psychotherapy: The Purchase of Friendship*. Englewood Cliffs, N.J.: Prentice-Hall, 1964.

SCHUMACHER, E. F. *Small Is Beautiful: Economics as if People Mattered*. New York: Harper & Row, 1973.

SCODEL, A. "Inspirational Group Therapy: A Study of Gamblers Anonymous." *American Journal of Psychotherapy*, 1964, *18*, 115–125.

SEAMAN, B. "Pelvic Autonomy: Four Proposals." *Social Policy*, 1975, *6*, 43–47.

SEHNERT, K. *How to Be Your Own Doctor (Sometimes)*. New York: Grossett & Dunlap, 1975.

SEHNERT, K. W., and OSTERWEIS, M. "The Activated Patient: A Concept for Health Education." *Continuing Education*, 1972, *17*, 52–56.

Self-Help and Health: A Report. New York: City Univerity of New York, Queens College, New Human Services Institute, 1976.

SERGIS, E., and HILGARTNER, M. "Hemophilia: Teaching Transfusion for Home Care." *American Journal of Nursing*, 1972, *72*, 92–93.

SIDEL, V. W., and SIDEL, R. "Beyond Coping." *Social Policy*, 1976, *7*, 67–69.

SILVERMAN, P. R. "The Widow as Care-Giver in a Program of Preventative Intervention with Other Widows: I Know What It Is Like. Let Me Help You." *Mental Hygiene*, 1970, *54*, 540–547.

SILVERMAN, P. R. "Factors Involved in Accepting an Offer of Help." *Archives of the Foundation for Thanatology*, 1971, *3*, 161–171.

SILVERMAN, P. R. "Widowhood and Preventive Integration." *Family Coordinator*, 1972, *21*, 95–102.

SILVERMAN, P. R., and MURROW, H. G. "Mutual Help During Critical Role Transitions." *Journal of Applied Behavioral Science*, 1976, *12*, 410–418.

SIMON, S. I. "Synanon: Towards Building a Humanistic Organization." Unpublished manuscript, Synanon, Tomales Bay, CA 94971, 1976.

SKOVHOLT, T. M. "The Client as Helper: A Means to Promote Psychological Growth." *Counseling Psychologist*, 1974, *4*, 58–64.

So You Have—Or Will Have an Ostomy. Los Angeles: United Ostomy Association, 1975.

SOMERS, A. R. "Community Health Education." *Journal of the Medical Society of New Jersey*, 1973, *70*, 943–948.

SOMERS, A. R. (Ed.) *Promoting Health: Consumer Education and National Policy*. Germantown, Md.: Aspen Systems, 1976.

"Special Self-Help Issue." *Social Policy*, 1976, *7*, 1–96.

STABLER, B., GIBSON, F. W., JR., and CUTTING, D. S. "Parents as Therapists: An Innovative Community-Based Model." *Professional Psychology*, 1973, *4*, 397–402.

STEINMAN, R., and TRAUNSTEIN, D. M. "Redefining Deviance: The Self-Help Challenge to the Human Services." *Journal of Applied Behavioral Science*, 1976, *12*, 347–362.

STEINMANN, M. "Crib Death: Too Many Clues?" *New York Times Magazine*, May 16, 1976, pp. 40–43.

STEWART, D. A. "The Dynamics of Fellowship as Illustrated in Alcoholics Anonymous." *Quarterly Journal of Studies on Alcohol*, 1955, *16*, 251–262.

STRAUSS, A. "Chronic Illness." *Society*, 1973, *10*, 26–36.

STUNKARD, A. J. "The Success of TOPS, a Self-Help Group." *Post-Graduate Medicine*, 1972, *18*, 143–147.

THELEN, H. A. "The Humane Person Defined." Paper presented at the Secondary Education Leadership Conference, St. Louis, Missouri, November 1967.

THELEN, H. A. "Learning by Teaching." Report of a conference on the Helping Relationship in the Classroom, Stone-Brandel Center, University of Chicago, 1968.

THOMSEN, R. *Bill W*. New York: Harper & Row, 1975.

TIEBOUT, H. M. "Therapeutic Mechanisms of AA." *American Journal of Psychiatry*, 1944, *100*, 468–473.

TOCH, H. *The Social Psychology of Social Movements*. New York: Bobbs-Merrill, 1965.

TORREY, E. F. *The Mind Game: Witchdoctors and Psychiatrists*. New York: Emerson Hall, 1972.

TRACY, G. S., and GUSSOW, Z. "Self-Help Groups: A Grassroots Response to a Need for Services." *Journal of Applied Behavioral Science*, 1976, *12*, 381–396.

TRICE, R. B. (Ed.). *The Sociology of Psychotherapy*. New York: Aronson, 1974.

TRUAX, C. B., and CARKHUFF, R. R. *Towards Effective Counseling and Psychotherapy*. Chicago: Aldine, 1973.

TYLER, R. W. "Social Policy and Self-Help Groups." *Journal of Applied Behavioral Science*, 1976, *12*, 444–448.

"United Ostomy Association, Inc." *The Exceptional Parent*, August 1975, pp. 28–29.

VAN STONE, W., and GILBERT, R. "Peer Confrontation Groups: What, Why, Whether." *American Journal of Psychiatry*, 1972, *129*, 583–588.

VATTANO, A. J. "Power to the People: Self-Help Groups." *Social Work*, 1972, *17*, 7–15.

VOLKMAN, R., and CRESSEY, D. "Differential Association and the Rehabilitation of Drug Addicts." *American Journal of Sociology*, 1963, *69*, 129–142.

W., BILL. *Alcoholics Anonymous Comes of Age*. New York: Harper & Row, 1957.

WAGONFELD, S., and WOLOWITZ, H. M. "Obesity and the Self-Help Group: A Look at TOPS." *American Journal of Psychiatry*, 1968, *125*, 249–252.

WAHLER, R. G. "Oppositional Children: A Quest for Parental Reinforcement Control." *Journal of Applied Behavior Analysis*, 1969, *2*, 159–170.

WECHSLER, H. "The Ex-Patient Organization: A Survey." *The Journal of Social Issues*, 1960a, *16*, 47–53.

WECHSLER, H. "The Self-Help Organization in the Mental Health Field: Recovery, Inc., A Case Study." *Journal of Nervous and Mental Disorders*, 1960b, *130*, 297–314.

WECHSLER, H. "Patterns of Membership in a Self-Help Organization in Mental Health." *Mental Hygiene*, 1961, *45*, 613–622.

WEINBERG, M. S. "The Problems of Midgets and Dwarfs and Organizational Remedies: A Study of the Little People of America." *Journal of Health and Social Behavior,* 1968, *9,* 65–72.

WEISS, R. S. "The Fund of Sociability." *Trans-Action,* 1969, *6,* 36–43.

WEISS, R. S. "The Contributions of an Organization of Single Parents to the Well-Being of Its Members." *Family Coordinator,* 1973, *22,* 321–326.

WEPPNEA, R. S. "Some Characteristics of an Ex-Addict Self-Help Therapeutic Community and Its Members." *British Journal of Addiction,* 1973, *26,* 73–79.

West Coast Sisters, How to Start Your Self-Help Clinic. Los Angeles: Feminist Women's Health Center, 1971.

WHITNEY, E. D. (Ed.). *World Dialogue on Alcohol and Drug Dependence.* Boston: Beacon, 1970.

WILKINS, B. "Chuck Dederich Still Rules Synanon, But Now He Has 1,300 Subjects and a $22 Million Empire." *People,* September 18, 1976, pp. 86–95.

YABLONSKY, L. *Synanon: The Tunnel Back.* New York: Macmillan, 1965.

ZUNKER, V. G., and BROWN, W. F. "Comparative Effectiveness of Student and Professional Counselors." *Personnel and Guidance Journal,* 1966, *44,* 738–743.

Index

plicated the consumer choices, the greater the consumer intensivity. Thus, some consumer inputs—for example, holding one's head still, opening one's mouth wide—are relatively uncomplicated, while others, such as in biofeedback, self-hypnosis, and transcendental meditation (TM), are much more complicated, requiring greater consumer intensivity.

Until now we have been talking largely or implicitly of the *quantity* of production, rather than the *quality* of the service. But consumer intensivity may have an important and fundamental effect on the quality of the work, whether it be education or healing. The human services depend heavily on the involvement and motivation of the consumer. Whether children learn depends, in the end, on their becoming involved, learning how to learn, becoming turned on, becoming won to learning. An individual's health, in the last analysis, depends mainly on what he or she does about maintaining it, preventing illness, and building positive health. And, in most of the behavior-related disorders, such as oversmoking, alcoholism, and drug taking, it is obvious that the consumer's self-involvement is decisive. There are countless other illustrations of this in sex therapy, parenting, psychotherapy, family planning, and recreation. In all these cases, the individual consumer's involvement powerfully affects the *quality* of the service product.

We hypothesize that consumer intensivity increases in a major way when the consumer functions as both a deliverer and a receiver of a service (either simultaneously or sequentially). This seems to be the case in most of the self-help groups. Thus an alcoholic in AA receives help and support from another AA (and the group), and also gives help to other members (and is part of the group). All members play the helping role at one time or another, and so are helped both in the helpee role and in the helper role. This situation is therefore highly consumer intensive.

Consumer intensivity, of course, occurs not only in mutual aid groups, but also in a great variety of other areas where consumer input is critical. In all of the so-called coping books, the consumer is obviously the decisive force in helping him- or herself, and the professional input is restricted to the book itself.

Patients contribute to their own health (the service product) when they give an accurate history, follow the regimen prescribed by the doctor, and report reactions promptly and accurately. Actually, health is a particularly significant area with regard to self-help activity. A patient who carefully follows a prescribed regimen is engaging in highly consumer-intensive behavior. For example, one doctor in Indiana is reported to have helped 4,000 patients to make self-examinations. The service he provides obviously is highly consumer intensive.

Emerging Forms of Health Care

In the last fifty years, the incidence of infectious illness has been reduced, largely as a result of improved food and of sanitary and housing conditions. However, in the longer lives that we live, we are subject, instead, to a broad range of chronic disorders, such as diabetes, mental illness, cancer, heart disorder, hypertension, arthritis, and emphysema. As we have noted, about 50 percent of the population now suffers from chronic illnesses, which account for 70 percent of all doctor visits. In addition, there are the behavior-related disorders that stem from speedy driving and from smoking, drinking, and taking drugs. The big health problems of our time arise from the fact that we overeat, oversmoke, overdrink, overdrive, oversit, overwork, overheat, and underexercise.

Self-help groups have also been developed for those who suffer from acute disorders that persist, as well as patients in the acute episodic phase of long-term disorders, such as strokes and heart attacks. Organizations such as Mended Hearts, Reach to Recovery, The Stroke Club, and Laryngectomy, Inc., help patients adjust to their new situation after an operation or to highly specific treatment for the acute phase of their illness. The laryngectomy group helps club members perfect speech techniques. Mastectomy, Inc., helps patients face the psychic, interpersonal, marital, and sexual problems associated with breast loss, as well as their fear that the cancer may recur. Stroke Club members help train the patient and the family to communicate through finger pressure. These consumer-initiated services are playing an enormous role in the rehabilitative process, and major health organizations (for example, the American Cancer Society and American Heart Association) are now sponsoring self-help clubs. One of the most important expressions of self-help in the health field, of course, is found in the feminist perspective.

Mental Health and Education

In mental health, the major problems of our times relate to feelings of alienation, isolation, and lack of identity—problems resulting in part from the breakdown of traditional small groups such as the family, community, and neighborhood. Small self-help units may play an important role in filling this vacuum. Other specific mental health problems relate to various forms of addiction, such as drugs and gambling. Here the self-help groups have played an important role and are frequently recommended by the traditional agencies as the treatment of choice. Other issues, such as the loneliness of widows, suicide-prone individuals, and parents without partners, and the special needs of women and men who have formed consciousness-raising groups are other areas for which the small group, mutual aid orientation appears beneficial.

Institutions may also be supplemented by this approach. The failure of the correctional system and difficulties of a postprison existence has led to organizations such as The Fortune Society for exoffenders, and various types of self-help groups have developed for delinquents. The trend toward deinstitutionalization in the mental health field has important implications for the mutual aid modality. As they move out into the community, former mental patients need organizations such as Recovery, Inc., and other types of small units to aid them in their adjustment and transition to everyday life. In the field of education, rap groups and peer counseling approaches have played useful roles in schools troubled by drug abuse problems, uncontrolled aggression, and identity issues. Moreover, one of the central educational problems in our schools is the need to *contact* and turn on (motivate) youngsters who have not been won to learning. Approaches such as children-teaching-children have demonstrated considerable success in dealing with the development of learning and emotional growth. And increased recognition of the needs of educationally handicapped children, as well as improved legislation, have been powered in large part by parents who have formed self-help groups and a large-scale self-help movement.

The recent concern for dealing with the emotional problems of the dying has led to special self-help units, usually attached to hospitals. Special problems related to sexism, racism, and ageism have led to a great variety of self-help activities ranging from the Gray Panthers to women's groups, youth hotlines, and cooperatives of all kinds. Concerns with parenting, aggression, and sex behavior have brought forth a great number of self-help books. In sum, self-help already has an impressive record of achievement in these spheres.

Dangers

While the self-help design has significant advantages, there are a number of dangers that should be considered and counteracted. One set of dangers relates to the professional caregiving system.

1. The self-help approach may be used as an argument for the further curtailment of the services.
2. It may be used to reduce professional and system responsibility (the consumer may be told to "clean your own streets" rather than to demand responsible service by the Sanitation Department).
3. The recent concern for accountability and evaluation may be watered down to mean no more than customer satisfaction, and the goal of finding and developing objective indices of service performance may be surrendered.
4. The self-help approach may be thoroughly coopted by the professional establishment, which could then use the form of self-help groups as appendages of traditional agencies.

A key question, then, concerns the type of relationship that will exist between the professional agency and the self-help group. Will the professional attempt to dominate and socialize the self-help group to existing professional norms, or will the self-help group be independent, relating cooperatively with the professional structure—and thereby significantly modifying a basic dependency relationship in our society?